gue
Club Guide
1975-76

QUEEN ANNE PRESS LONDON

Compiled by Leslie Vernon and Jack Rollin

Published by Queen Anne Press Limited
12 Vandy Street, London EC2A 2EN

Typeset in Monotype Grotesque and printed
and bound in England by
Hazell Watson & Viney Ltd,
Aylesbury, Bucks

Contents

Introduction

As a companion to the now established Rothmans Football Yearbook, which is in its sixth year, we are presenting the *Rothmans Football League Club Guide 1975–76*.

This handy pocket-size publication should prove invaluable to supporters both at their home club and when visiting other grounds. Information both written and visual will help plan ahead for a trip to an unfamiliar location.

For each of the 92 League clubs, plus Wembley Stadium, there is a diagram of the ground showing the exact siting of terraces and stands as well as adjacent roads. The main bus and train routes are noted along with information on car parking facilities in the vicinity.

Supporters wishing to know the best way to apply for tickets will find these details along with notes concerning entertainment and catering facilities at the ground and the whereabouts of any club shop.

In addition to the fixtures for the four divisions of the Football League, a list of international and representative matches is also included which should provide an extra facility in preparing an itinerary for the 1975–76 season.

European, International, and Cup dates 1975–76

AUGUST 1975
9 Charity Shield, Derby Co. v. West Ham U.; **20** League Cup 1st Round; **30** FA Cup Preliminary Round.

SEPTEMBER 1975
3 Switzerland v England (Friendly), Denmark v Scotland (European Championship), N. Ireland v Sweden (European Championship); **10** League Cup 2nd Round; **13** FA Cup 1st Round qualifying; **17** European Cups 1st Round (1st leg); **20** FA Challenge Trophy Preliminary Round.

OCTOBER 1975
1 European Cups 1st Round (2nd leg); **4** FA Cup 2nd Round qualifying; **8** League Cup 3rd Round; **11** FA Challenge Trophy 1st Round qualifying; **18** FA Cup 3rd Round qualifying; **22** European Cups 2nd Round (1st leg); **28** Czechoslovakia v England (Under-23); **29** Czechoslovakia v England (European Championship), Scotland v Denmark (European Championship), N. Ireland v Norway (European Championship), Eire v Turkey (European Championship).

NOVEMBER 1975
1 FA Cup 4th Round qualifying; **5** European Cups 2nd Round (2nd leg); **8** FA Challenge Trophy 2nd Round qualifying; **12** League Cup 4th Round; **19** Portugal v England (European Championship), Yugoslavia v N. Ireland (European Championship), Wales v Austria (European Championship), England v Portugal (Under-23); **20** Turkey v Eire (European Championship); **22** FA Cup 1st Round; **26** UEFA Cup 3rd Round (1st leg); **29** FA Challenge Trophy 3rd Round qualifying.

DECEMBER 1975
3 League Cup 5th Round; **10** UEFA Cup 3rd Round (2nd leg); **13** FA Cup 2nd Round; **17** Scotland v Rumania (European Championship).

JANUARY 1976
3 FA Cup 3rd Round; **10** FA Challenge Trophy 1st Round; **14** League Cup semi-final (1st leg); **21** League Cup semi-final (2nd leg); **24** FA Cup 4th Round; **31** FA Challenge Trophy 2nd Round.

FEBRUARY 1976
14 FA Cup 5th Round; **21** FA Challenge Trophy 3rd Round; **28** League Cup final.

MARCH 1976
3 European Cups quarter-finals (1st leg); **6** FA Cup 6th Round, FA Challenge Trophy 4th Round; **17** European Cups quarter-finals (2nd leg); **27** FA Challenge Trophy semi-finals (1st leg); **31** European Cups semi-finals (1st leg).

APRIL 1976
3 FA Cup semi-finals, FA Challenge Trophy semi-finals (2nd leg); **10** FA Challenge Vase final; **14** European Cups semi-finals (2nd leg); **24** FA Challenge Trophy final, European Championship quarter-finals (1st leg); **25** FA Sunday Cup final; **28** UEFA Cup final (1st leg), FA Youth Cup final (1st leg).

MAY 1976
1 FA Cup final; **5** European Cup-Winners' Cup final; **6** British International Championship; **12** British International Championship, European Cup final; **15** British International Championship; **19** UEFA Cup final (2nd leg), FA Youth Cup final (2nd leg); **22** European Championship quarter-finals (2nd leg).

JUNE 1976
16–20 (Provisional dates) European Championship semi-finals and final.

ALDERSHOT

RECREATION GROUND: HIGH ST., ALDERSHOT.

TELEPHONE ALDERSHOT 20211.

Ground capacity: 20,000 (18,000 under cover). **Pitch measurements:** 117 yds × 76 yds. **Address of Supporters Club:** 127 High Street, Aldershot.

How to get there: Aldershot railway station is on the main line from London's Waterloo; the ground is five minutes walk from the station. Many buses run from the town centre on match days.

Match tickets: Can be booked 2 weeks in advance by telephoning ground.

Car parking: Car parks within ¾ mile of the ground. A park at the ground is in the process of being levelled.

Entertainments/catering facilities: Members' club.

Club shop: Run by Supporters' Club; sells all types of souvenirs.

Handbooks/programmes: Programmes only available on sale.

Club colours: Red with blue trim, white shorts, red and blue socks.

Change Colours: Canary yellow shirts, blue shorts, yellow socks.

Club Nickname: 'Shots'.

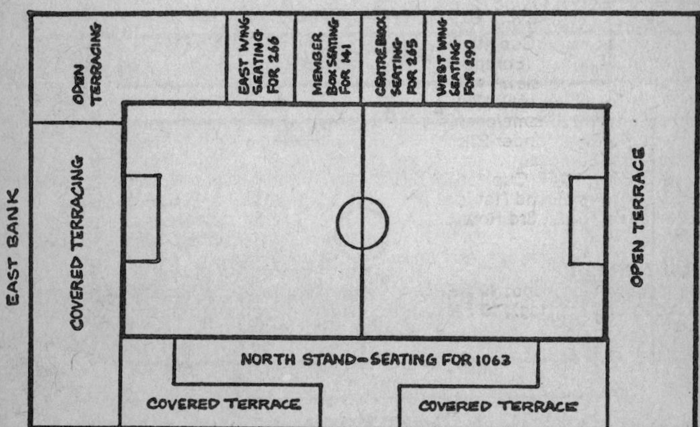

ARSENAL

ARSENAL STADIUM, HIGHBURY, LONDON N.5.

TELEPHONE 01-226-0304.

Telegraphs: 'Gunneretic London N.5.'

Ground capacity: 60,000. **Pitch measurements:** 110 yds × 71 yds.

How to get there: Arsenal Underground Station (Piccadilly Line) is within one minute of the ground. Finsbury Park (Piccadilly and Victoria) and Drayton Park (Northern) are also within walking distance. Buses 4a, 19, 106, 141a, 236.

Match tickets: Postal application 21 days prior to the match. Prices and availability of tickets can be checked with the club on their Ansafone Service (01)-359-0131.

Car parking: Parking is allowed in the adjacent streets under the control of the Police.

Entertainments/catering facilities: West Stand restaurant is open Mon.-Fri. for the general public and on match days for ticket holders in the West Stand Upper tier. East Stand restaurant is open on match days only for ticket holders in the East Stand Upper tier. Reservations for both restaurants can be made by telephoning (01)-226-4968. There are also extensive refreshment bars around the ground.

Club shop: Shop in Avenell Road, Highbury, is open Mon.-Fri. 9.30 am.–5 pm. On Saturday first team matches it is open from 1.00 pm.–5.30 pm. Other shops in the ground are open on match days.

Handbooks/programmes: Handbooks and programmes can be obtained from the club shop. Programmes available on subscription.

Club Colours: Red shirts with white sleeves, white shorts, red and white stockings.

Change Colours: Yellow shirts with blue shorts, yellow stockings.

Club Nickname: 'Gunners'.

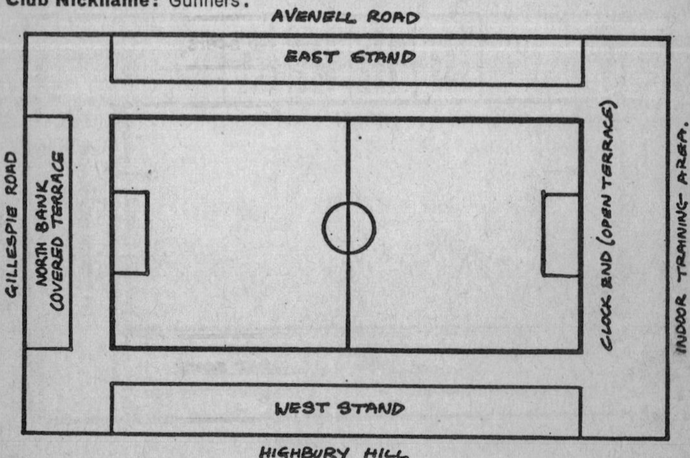

ASTON VILLA

VILLA PARK, TRINITY RD., BIRMINGHAM 6.

TELEPHONE 021-327 6604.

Telegraphic Address: 'Villa, Birmingham 6'.

Ground capacity: 58,250. **Pitch measurements:** 115 yds × 75 yds. **Address of Supporters Club:** c/o Villa ground.

How to get there: Bus 5 from Corporation Street to Witton Square. Special buses from Priory Ringway and Hall of Memory (city centre). Birmingham New Street railway station is near the centre. The ground is ½ mile from link to the motorway.

Match tickets: Postal applications one month in advance, personal applications two weeks in advance.

Car parking: Serpentine Car Park in Aston Hall Road. Side-street parking also available.

Entertainments/catering facilities: Lions Club (members only) adjacent to the ground. Many refreshment points around the ground.

Club Shop: Adjacent to the ground; sells all types of souvenirs.

Handbooks/programmes: Programmes available on seasonal subscription.

Club Colours: Claret shirts with light blue sleeves, blue shorts, white stockings.

Change Colours: Blue and yellow.

Club Nickname: 'Villans'.

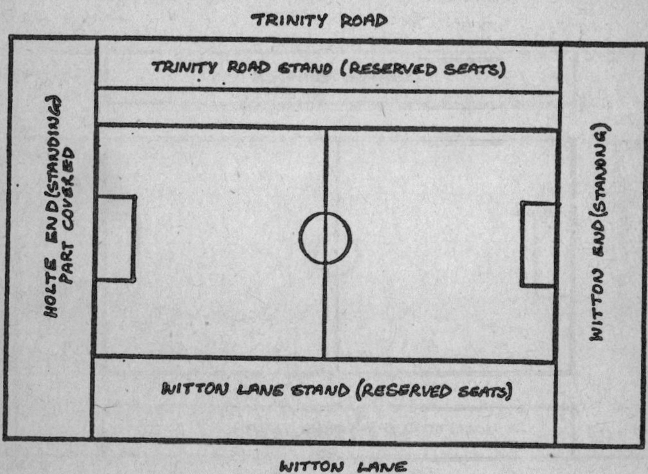

BARNSLEY

OAKWELL GROUND, GROVE ST., BARNSLEY:

TELEPHONE BARNSLEY 84113.

Ground capacity: 38,500 (15,000 under cover). **Pitch measurements:** 111 yds × 75 yds.

How to get there: Fairly frequent train service from Sheffield and Leeds to Exchange Station Barnsley. No special buses, just the normal services, and no buses from town centre because the ground is so close.

Match tickets: Stand seats bookable two weeks in advance.

Car parking: Official club park adjacent to the ground holds 600 cars; parking fee 5p. The Yorkshire Traction Company Park, also adjacent, holds another 800 at the same fee. There is a free public park in Queens Road, two minutes from the ground. The M1 runs approximately two miles from the ground.

Entertainments/catering facilities: Football club social club is adjacent to the ground. Seven tea bars sited around the ground sell hot drinks and pies; six of them sell alcoholic drinks.

Club shop: Inside the ground, sells all types of souvenirs.

Handbooks/programmes: Programmes available on subscription.

Club Colours: Red shirts, white shorts, white stockings.

Change Colours: All white or yellow and blue.

Club Nickname: 'The Tykes'.

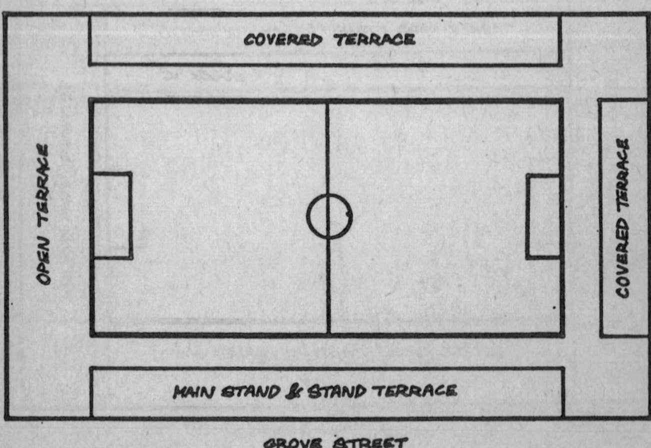

BIRMINGHAM CITY

ST. ANDREWS, BIRMINGHAM B9 4NH.

TELEPHONE 021-772 0101/2689.

Telegraphic Address: 'Heathen Birmingham'.

Ground capacity: 52,500 (9,579 seats). **Pitch measurements:** 115 yds × 75 yds.

Address of Supporters Club: St. Andrew's Club, St. Andrew's, Birmingham 9.

How to get there: Buses 53, 54 from Carr's Lane, City Centre. Specials from Albert Street and Hall of Memory, Broad Street. Nearest railway station, Birmingham New Street. By road; via M1, M45, and A45 to Small Heath area of Birmingham and via Cattell Road (sixth turning on the right past Small Heath Park) to the ground; via M6 (exit 6, Gravelly Hill) and A38M (Aston Expressway), leave Expressway at first exit, left into Dartmouth Street, and then via Lawley Street and Watery Lane onto the Coventry Road. Turn left and then take left fork into Cattell Road.

Match tickets: Bookable three weeks in advance.

Car parking: Public car park in Garrison Lane.

Entertainments/catering facilities: Catering points inside the ground.

Club shop: Sells all types of souvenirs.

Handbooks/programmes: Programmes on sale on match days in and outside the ground; subscription rates available on request.

Club Colours: Royal blue shirts, with broad white vertical stripe, white collars and cuffs, white shorts, blue stockings.

Change Colours: Red shirts, white shorts, red and white stockings.

Club Nickname: 'Blues'.

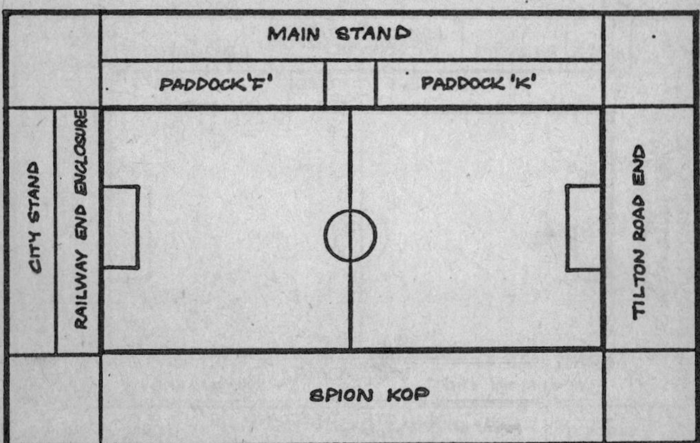

BLACKBURN ROVERS

EWOOD PARK, BLACKBURN BB2 4JF.
TELEPHONE BLACKBURN 55432/55433.
Telegraphic Address: 'Rovers, Blackburn'.
Ground capacity: 47,500. **Pitch measurements:** 116 yds 2 ft × 72 yds 2 ft.

How to get there: Blackburn is the nearest railway station and Corporation buses run from there to the ground.
Match tickets: Seats can be booked 14 days in advance.
Car parking: Ample street parking around the ground.
Entertainments/catering facilities: Licensed refreshment bars in all parts of the ground.
Club shop: Open on match days selling all types of souvenirs.
Handbook/programmes: No handbook. Programmes available on subscription from the club shop.
Club Colours: Blue and white halved shirts, white shorts, blue stockings with two white rings.
Change Colours: Red and black striped shirts, black shorts, black stockings with red and white tops.
Club Nickname: 'Blue and Whites'.

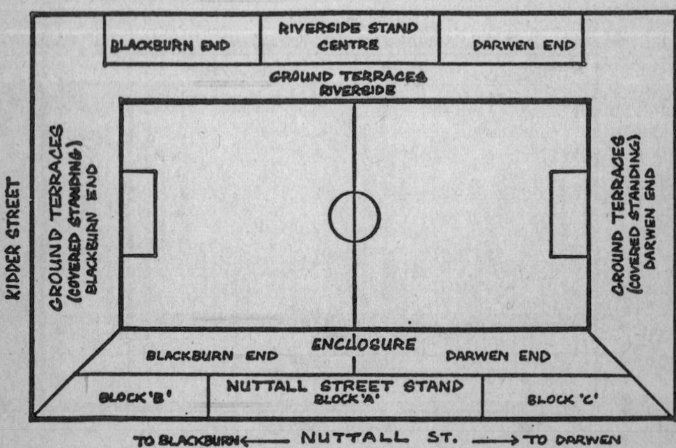

BLACKPOOL

BLOOMFIELD RD. GROUND, BLACKPOOL FY1 6JJ.

TELEPHONE BLACKPOOL 46118.

Telegraphic address: 'Football Blackpool'.

Ground capacity: 38,000. **Pitch measurements:** 111 yds × 73 yds. **Address of Supporters Club:** Blackpool F.C., Development Association, Bloomfield Road, Blackpool, Lancs.

How to get there: Coliseum bus station, Lytham Road, 10 minutes' walk. Railway: South station (a few minutes' walk from ground) and North station.

Match tickets: Bookable four weeks in advance of the match.

Car parking: Car park for 100–120 cars. Street parking available.

Entertainments/catering facilities: Refreshment and licensed bars. Entertainment after the game at the Supporters' Club by prior arrangement.

Club shop: In Bloomfield Road, sells all types of souvenirs.

Handbooks/programmes: Programmes available from the Supporters' Club and development shop.

Club Colours: Tangerine shirts with white collars and cuffs, white shorts, tangerine stockings.

Change Colours: White shirts, tangerine shorts and white stockings.

Club Nickname: 'The Tangerines'.

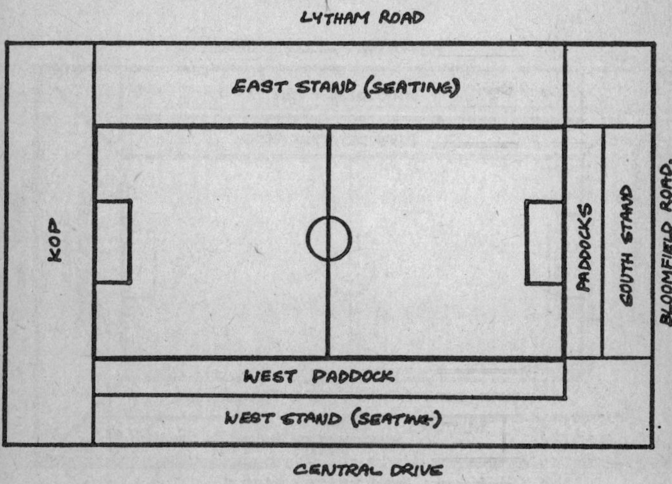

BOLTON WANDERERS

BURNDEN PARK, BOLTON, BL3 2WR.

TELEPHONE BOLTON 21101.

Ground capacity: 60,136. **Pitch measurements:** 113 yds× 76 yds. **Address of Supporters Club:** Supporters Club, Burnden Park, Manchester Road, Bolton.

How to get there: Local buses 8, 524, 523, 542, 543. The nearest station is Trinity St. in the town centre.

Match tickets: Bookable two weeks in advance.

Car parking: Private car parking only on Burnden forecourt. Large park only 200 yards from the ground. Limited street parking in the vicinity. Multi-storey parks in the town centre.

Entertainments/catering facilities: Prerecorded programmes of news, interviews, and record requests. Burnden Sporting Club open before matches and cabarets there on Friday and Saturday evenings. Refreshment bars in each section of the ground and in the Sporting Club.

Club shop: Open match days only. Postal applications and price lists available on request.

Handbooks/programmes: Programmes available on subscription from club shop.

Club Colours: White shirts, dark blue shorts, white stockings.

Change Colours: Red shirts, white trimmings, blue shorts.

Club Nickname: 'Trotters'.

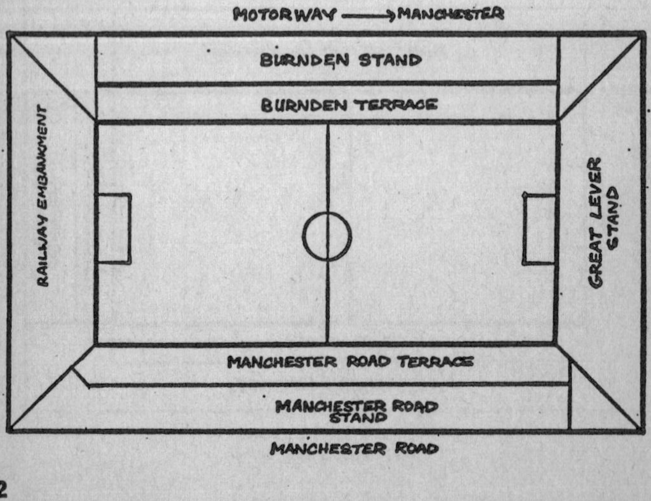

AFC BOURNEMOUTH

DEAN COURT GROUND, BOURNEMOUTH.

TELEPHONE BOURNEMOUTH 35381.

Telegraphic address: 'Football Bournemouth.'

Ground capacity: 24,000. **Pitch measurements:** 115 × 75 yds. **Address of Supporters Club Shop.** The Cherry Bees Shop, Dean Court, Bournemouth, Hants.

How to get there: Nearest railway station Bournemouth Central on the main line from London (Waterloo). Corporation bus 25.

Match tickets: Seats can be booked 10 days in advance by telephone, personal application, or post.

Car parking: Adequate parking for 1500 cars.

Entertainments/catering facilities: Refreshment points around the ground.

Club shop: Sells all types of souvenirs.

Handbooks/programmes: No handbook. Programmes available on subscription.

Club Colours: Red shirts with white trim, white shorts, black stockings with red and white tops.

Change Colours: All white with red trim on shirts.

Club Nickname: 'Cherries'.

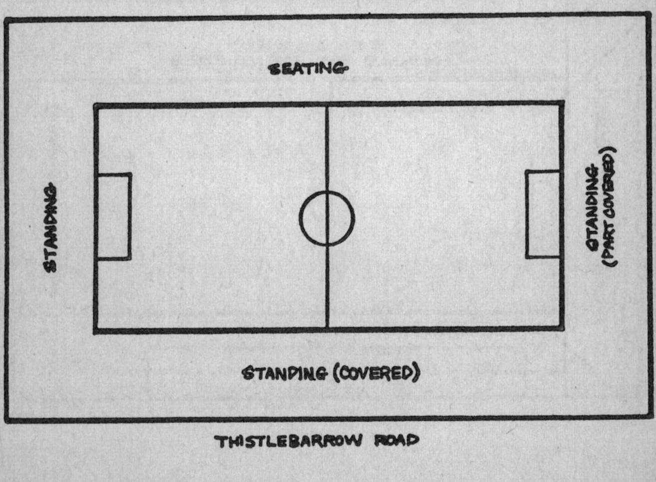

BRADFORD CITY

VALLEY PARADE GROUND, BRADFORD BO8 7OY.

TELEPHONE BRADFORD 26565.

Ground capacity: 23,469. **Pitch measurements:** 110 yds × 70 yds. **Address of Supporters Club:** c/o Football Club.

How to get there: Ground situated approximately $\frac{3}{4}$ mile from city centre along Manningham Lane. Corporation buses 23–26 from Cheapside plus specials. West Yorkshire buses from Chester St. bus station. The nearest railway station is Bradford Exchange. By road, the ground is approximately $\frac{1}{4}$ mile from Ring Road towards Bradford.

Match tickets: Booking in advance from 14 days prior to the match; bookings cease 3 hours before kick-off. Postal applications should include remittance and S.A.E.

Car parking: Club car park off Valley Parade holds 100 cars. Street parking in most side-streets. No parking in Valley Parade or South Parade.

Entertainments/catering facilities: Members' club adjacent to ground; this admits adult members of visiting supporters' clubs on production of members' card. Hot drinks, pies, crisps, etc available at snack bars in the ground.

Club shop: Adjacent to ground entrance; sells all types of souvenirs.

Handbooks/programmes: Programmes will be sent on receipt of remittance and S.A.E.

Club Colours: All white with claret and amber stripes, trim.

Change Colours: Amber shirts, claret shorts.

Club Nickname: 'The Paraders'.

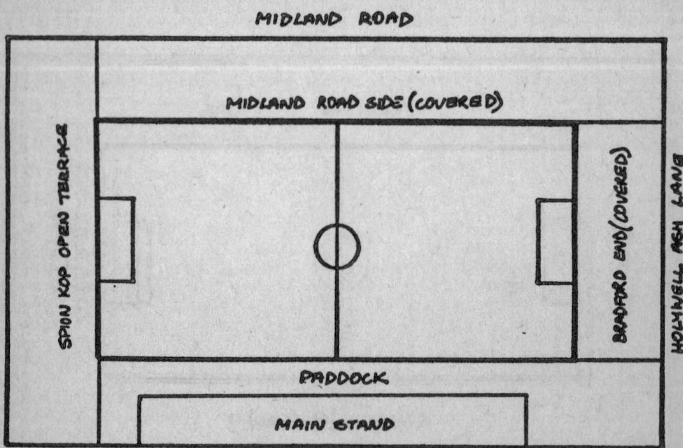

BRENTFORD

GRIFFIN PARK, BRAEMER RD., BRENTFORD, MIDDLESEX TW8 ONT.
TELEPHONE 01-560-2021.

Ground capacity: 37,000 (30,500 under cover). **Pitch measurements:** 114 yds × 75 yds. **Address of Supporters Club:** Same as Football Club.

How to get there: South Ealing (Underground, Piccadilly line). Southern Region trains from Waterloo to Brentford Central. Buses 91, 65, 116, 117, E1, E2, 267. The ground is within a mile of the M4 and A4 roads.

Match tickets: All admission by cash through turnstiles. Only Cup-tie seats may be booked.

Car parking: Mainly confined to streets around the ground. A small park at Ealing Road entrance and a larger one at the junction of Brook Road and Clifden Road; charges 15–20p. Access to the latter may be gained only by the gate in Clifden Road approaching from the Boston Manor Road end.

Entertainments/catering facilities: Catering kiosks and licensed bars in the ground. A members' social club, the Bees Club in Braemer Road, provides entertainment throughout the year.

Club-shop: The Supporters' Club sells all souvenir items. Applications for price lists, etc should be sent to the Sales Secretary, Brentford Football Supporters & Social Club, c/o Brentford F.C., accompanied by S.A.E.

Handbook/programmes: Programmes not available on subscription.

Club Colours: Red and white striped shirts, black shorts.

Change Colours: Yellow shirts with blue trim, blue shorts, yellow stockings with blue tops.

Club Nickname: 'Bees'.

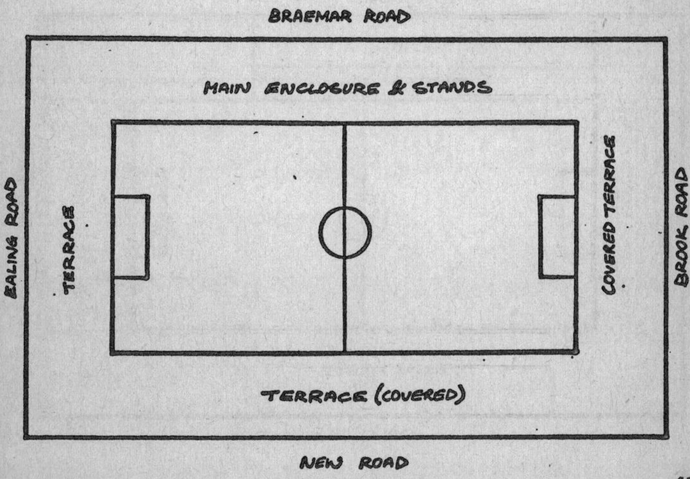

BRIGHTON & HOVE ALBION

GOLDSTONE GROUND, OLD SHOREHAM RD., HOVE, EAST SUSSEX, BN3 7DE.

TELEPHONE BRIGHTON 739535.

Ground capacity: 38,000. **Pitch measurements:** 112 yds × 75 yds. **Address of Supporters Club:** Albion Shop, Goldstone Ground, Hove.

How to get there: Buses 5, B5, 26, 40, 55, 19 from Old Steyne and 11 via Brighton station and Old Shoreham Rd. Hove station is five minutes walk from the ground.

Match tickets: Postal bookings for tickets three weeks in advance.

Car parking: Street parking plus large car park at the nearby Greyhound Stadium.

Entertainments/catering facilities: Bars and tea stands around the ground.

Club shop: At the ground; sells all types of souvenirs.

Handbook/programmes: Programmes available by post from the club shop.

Club Colours: Blue and white striped shirts, blue shorts, blue stockings.

Change Colours: Yellow shirts, blue shorts, yellow stockings.

Club Nickname: 'The Albion' or 'The Dolphins'.

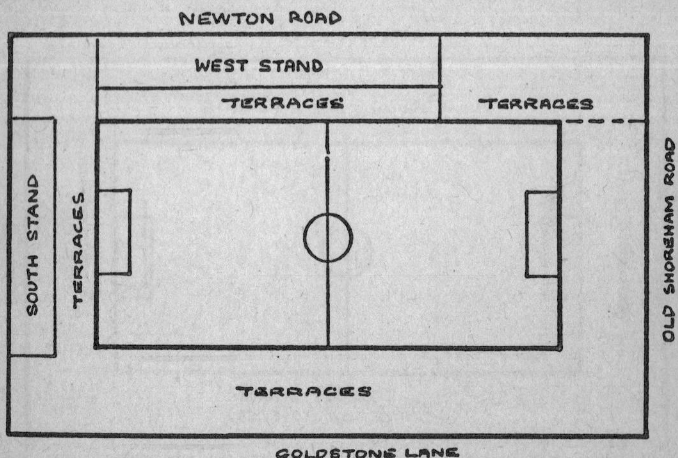

BRISTOL CITY

ASHTON GATE, BRISTOL BS3 2EJ.

TELEPHONE BRISTOL 664093 and 665428.

Telegraphic address: 'City Bristol'.

Ground capacity: 37,000. **Pitch measurements:** 115 yds × 75 yds. **Address of Supporters Club:** Supporters Club, Bristol City F.C., Ashton Gate, Bristol BS3 2EJ.

How to get there: Buses 6, 7, 9, 19, 22. Parson St. railway station is within walking distance. By special arrangement Ashton Gate station is open to visiting supporters' trains.

Match tickets: Tickets can be booked any length of time before the match; they will be issued 14 days prior to kick-off. Postal application must include remittance and S.A.E. Seats can also be reserved by personal application or by telephone; tickets booked by telephone must be collected 30 minutes before the start of the game.

Car parking: Season-ticket holders park at the ground. Coaches can park in the ground for 25p. Ample street parking around the ground.

Entertainments/catering facilities: Social club in the main stand. Tea bars in the ground. Alcoholic beverages only available to bona fide members of supporters clubs.

Club shop: Run by the Supporters' Club; sells all types of souvenirs.

Handbooks/programmes: Supporters' Club produce a handbook. Programmes not available on subscription but postal appliations are accepted.

Club Colours: Red shirts, white shorts, red stockings.

Change Colours: All white.

Club Nickname: 'Robins'.

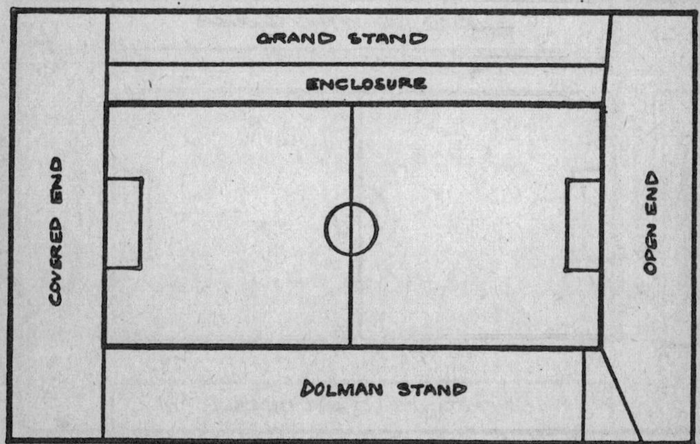

BRISTOL ROVERS

BRISTOL STADIUM, EASTVILLE, BRISTOL BS5 6NN.
TELEPHONE BRISTOL 558620.

Ground capacity: 39,333 (21,000 covered). **Pitch measurements:** 112 yds × 76 yds. **Address of Supporters Club:** 468 Stapleton Road, Bristol.

How to get there: Buses 44, 45, 11 from Temple Meads Station to Stapleton Rd., five minutes from ground. By car, leave M4 or M5 at M32 junction; M32 runs direct to the ground.

Match tickets: Stand tickets available two weeks prior to the match.

Car Parking: Large car parks at Stapleton Rd. and Muller Rd. entrances.

Entertainments/catering facilities: Bars open to the public in both stands. Tea bars on the terraces.

Club shop: In Stapleton Rd.; sells all types of souvenirs.

Handbooks/programmes: Handbooks and programmes available from club shop; programmes can be ordered on subscription.

Club Colours: Blue and white quartered shirts, white shorts, blue stockings with a white band at top.

Change Colours: White shirts, black shorts and red stockings.

Club Nickname: 'The Pirates'.

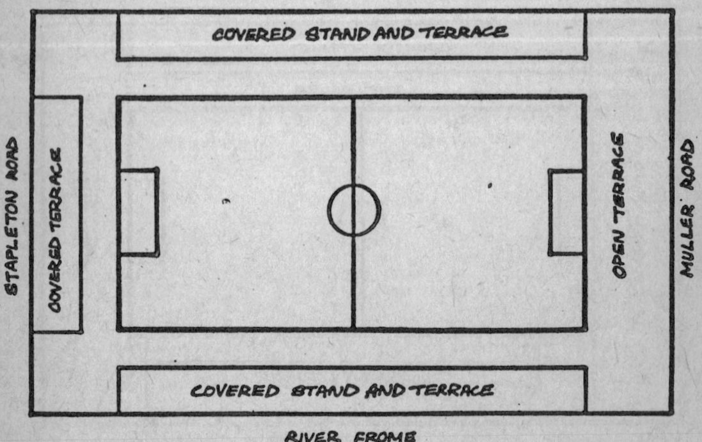

BURNLEY

TURF MOOR, BURNLEY.

TELEPHONES: OFFICE: BURNLEY (0282) 27777. TICKET OFFICE AND SHOP: BURNLEY 27777.

Ground capacity: 41,0000 **Pitch measurements:** 115 yds × 73 yds.

How to get there: Central bus station and the Central railway station are both within 10 minutes walk of the ground, which is near the town centre.

Match tickets: Reserved seats £1.75, £1.25, £1.00. Pre-match bookings one month in advance.

Car parking: Parks in Church St. and Fulledge Recreation Ground are both chargeable. Each holds about 500 cars.

Entertainments/catering facilities: Snack and licensed bars are sited around the ground; also 'chippy and hamburger' bars.

Club shop: Attached to the Development Office in Brunshaw Rd., Burnley. Telephone: Burnley 22720.

Handbooks/programmes: No handbooks. There is a subscription list for League programmes on a seasonal basis; enquiries c/o Club shop.

Club Colours: Claret shirts with blue cuffs, white shorts and stockings.

Change Colours: White shirts, claret shorts, blue stockings.

Club Nickname: 'Clarets'.

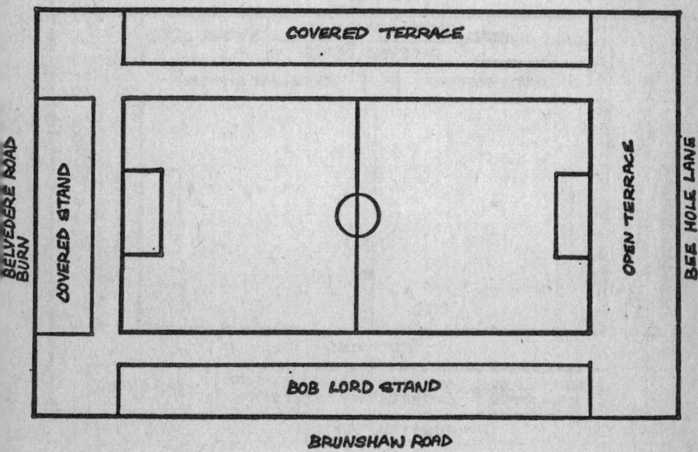

BURY

GIGG LANE, BURY BL9 9HR.

TELEPHONE 061-764 4881/2.

Ground caacity: 35,000. **Pitch measurements:** 112 yds × 72 yds.

How to get there: Buses 1, 2, 29, 35, 37, 38, 48, 52 from Kay Gardens to within walking distance. The nearest railway station is Bolton St. Buses run from the station to the ground.

Match tickets: 500 seats in the Reserved Chair section of the main stand may be booked two weeks before the match.

Car parking: Season-ticket holders only may use the car park on match days. But there is ample parking space in the side-streets around the ground.

Entertainments/catering facilities: Social club open during normal licensing hours.

Club shop: At the ground; sells all types of souvenirs.

Handbooks/programmes: Programmes available from club shop.

Club Colours: White shirts, royal blue shorts, royal blue stockings with white band.

Change Colours: Yellow shirts, royal blue shorts, yellow stockings.

Club Nickname: 'Shakers'.

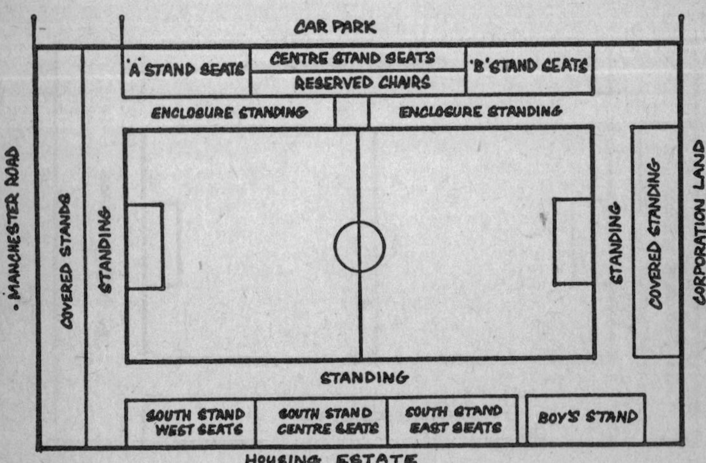

CAMBRIDGE UNITED

ABBEY STADIUM, NEWMARKET RD., CAMBRIDGE.

TELEPHONE TEVERSHAM (02205) 2170.

Ground capacity: 12,000. **Pitch measurements:** 115yds × 75 yds. **Address of Supporters Club:** 530, Newmarket Rd., Cambridge.

How to get there: Nearest railway station; Cambridge. Buses 180 and 181 run from the station to the town centre; then buses 182 and 183 to the ground, which is situated on the east side of the city.

Match tickets: Reserved seats bookable 14 days in advance. Postal applications must be accompanied by remittance and S.A.E.

Car parking: Limited parking at main entrance; off-street parking allowed, and at Coldhams Common.

Entertainments/catering facilities: Entertainments each evening organised by Supporters' Club. Three canteens open in the ground on match days.

Club shop: Two shops, one at the main entrance, the other inside the ground.

Handbooks/programmes: Handbooks not available.

Club Colours: Amber shirts with black collar and cuffs, black shorts, amber stockings.

Change Colours: White.

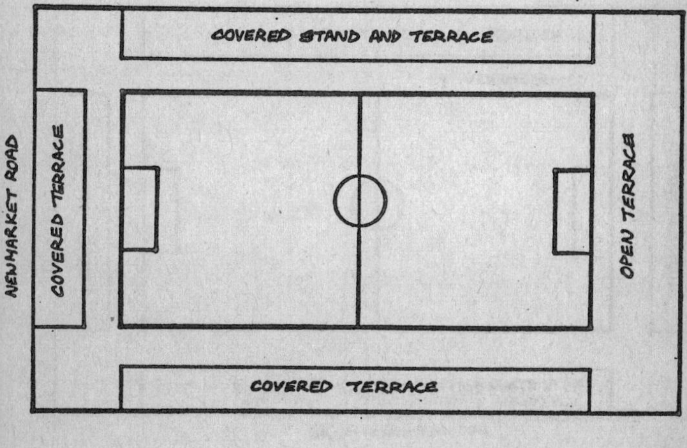

CARDIFF CITY

NINIAN PARK, CARDIFF CF1 8SX.

TELEPHONE CARDIFF 28501/33230.

Telegraphic address: 'Soccer Cardiff'.

Ground capacity: 47,000. **Pitch measurements:** 112 yds × 76 yds. **Address of Supporters Club:** Bluebirds Club, Bluebirds Office, Ninian Park, Cardiff CF1 8SX.

How to get there: Corporation bus 37 runs past the ground; special buses run to Ninian Park from the bus station, returning after the match. Nearest railway station, Cardiff General.

Match tickets: Bookable 14 days in advance by postal application. Details from Ticket Office (tel: Cardiff 397997).

Entertainments/catering facilities: Visiting supporters welcome at the Bluebirds Club on production of their supporters' club card or a rail or bus ticket. Refreshment points around the ground (licence being applied for).

Club shop: Open on match days; souvenirs available during the week from the Pools Office.

Handbooks/programmes: No handbook. Back numbers of programmes available from Programme Dept., Ninian Park.

Club Colours: Blue shirts, white shorts and stockings.

Change Colours: All yellow.

Club Nickname: 'Bluebirds'.

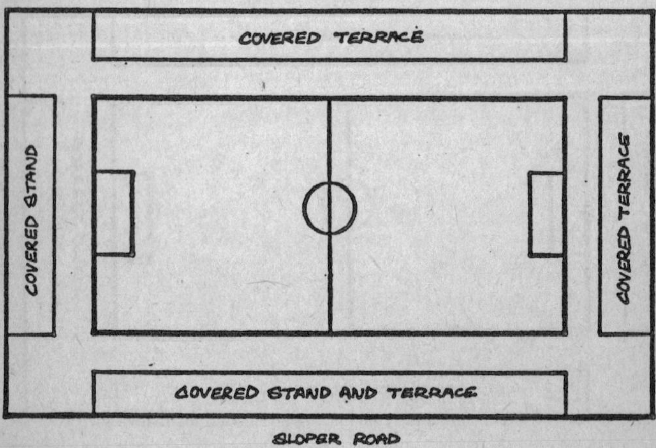

CARLISLE UNITED

BRUNTON PARK, CARLISLE, CA1 1LL.

TELEPHONE CARLISLE 26237

Ground capacity: 25,500. **Pitch measurements:** 117 yds × 78 yds.

How to get there: City centre one mile away, Ribble buses from the Town Hall. Nearest railway station Carlisle. By road—exit 43 from the M6, ground ¾ mile away; this avoids the town centre.

Match tickets: Bookable 1–2 weeks in advance by post or personal application.

Car parking: Car park holding 1500 vehicles adjacent to the ground. Limited street parking available.

Entertainments/catering facilities: Supporters Club with extensive bar facilities. Refreshment points around the ground.

Club shop: Caravan in car park open on match days.

Handbooks/programmes: No handbook. Programmes available on subscription.

Club Colours: Blue shirts, white shorts, blue stockings.

Change Colours: Yellow shirts, blue shorts, yellow stockings.

Club Nickname: 'Cumbrians'.

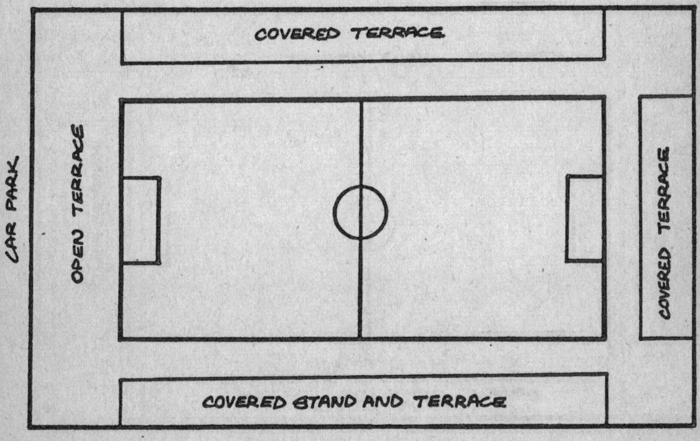

CHARLTON ATHLETIC

THE VALLEY, FLOYD RD., CHARLTON, LONDON SE7 8AW.

TELEPHONE 01-858-3711/2.

Ground capacity: 66,000 (largest capacity in Football League). **Pitch measurements:** 112 yds × 73 yds. **Address of Supporters Club:** Same address as Club.

How to get there: Buses 53, 54, 75, 177, 180. Nearest railway station, Charlton, is on the line from London from Charing Cross and Waterloo East. The ground is 3 minutes walk from the station.

Match tickets: Advance bookings for seats restricted to all Cup matches and selected League games.

Car parking: In ground for season-ticket holders only. Ample off-street parking available.

Entertainments/catering facilities: The Valley Club, Harvey Gardens, and Beer and Snack Bars in the ground.

Club shop: The Valley Shop in ground is open on match days.

Handbooks/programmes: Both available in shops, and programmes on subscription.

Club Colours: Red shirts, white shorts.

Change Colours: White and black.

Club Nickname: 'Haddicks', 'Robins', or 'Valiants'.

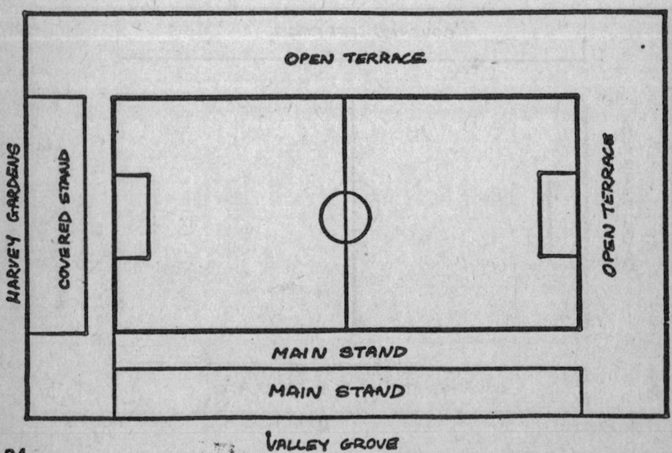

CHELSEA

STAMFORD BRIDGE, LONDON S.W.6.

TELEPHONE 01-385-5545/6.

Telegraphic address: 'Chelstam, London S.W.6.'

Ground capacity: 60,000 (31,500 covered).

Pitch measurements: 114 yds × 71 yds. **Address of Supporters Club:** Same as Football Club.

How to get there: Nearest station is Fulham Broadway on the Underground (District Line), London Transport regular buses to Fulham Broadway, Kings Road, Fulham Road, or Stamford Bridge.

Match tickets: Advance tickets available by postal or personal application. No telephone bookings.

Car parking: Street parking only.

Entertainments/catering facilities: Licensed bars at all points of the ground.

Club shop: Run by the Football Club; sells all types of souvenirs.

Handbooks/programmes: Programmes available on subscription. The club also produces an annual magazine.

Club Colours: All royal blue with white stripe on shorts. White stockings.

Change Colours: Red shirts, white shorts, green stockings.

Club Nickname: 'Blues'.

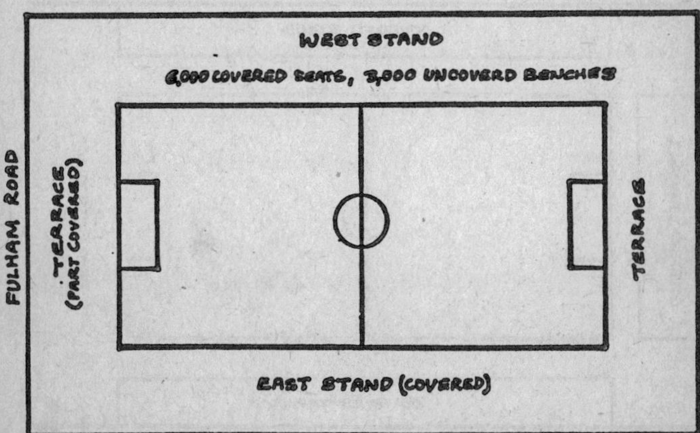

CHESTER

THE STADIUM, SEALAND RD., CHESTER CH1 4LW.
TELEPHONE CHESTER 21048.

Ground capacity: 20,000. **Pitch measurements:** 114 yds × 76 yds. **Address of Supporters Club:** 7 Bridge Street Row, Chester.

How to get there: Nearest railway station, Chester General. Corporation bus to Town Hall Square, where special buses run from the Odeon Cinema to the ground.

Match tickets: No advance booking.

Car parking: Extensive parking at ground.

Entertainments/catering facilities: Catering facilities on ground.

Club shop: In town centre: stocks all types of souvenirs.

Handbooks/programmes: Programmes not available on subscription.

Club Colours: Royal blue shirts with white stripes. White shorts.

Change Colour: Yellow shirts white shorts.

Club Nickname: 'The Seals'.

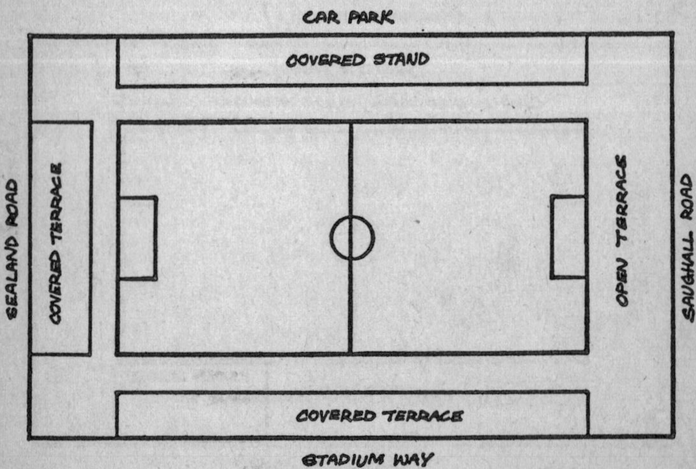

CHESTERFIELD

RECREATION GROUND, CHESTERFIELD.

TELEPHONE CHESTERFIELD 2318.

Ground capacity: 28,500 (12,000 covered). **Pitch measurements:** 114 yds × 72 yds.

How to get there: Chesterfield railway station is one mile from the ground, via Corporation St., Holywell St., to Saltergate.

Match tickets: Seats in the Centre and Wing Stands may be booked in advance.

Car parking: Street parking permitted around the ground. Also car parks in Saltergate within ½ mile of the ground.

Entertainments/catering facilities: A social club is sited on the ground at the Saltergate entrance. Entertainment provided at the Carlton Club and the Aquaries Club.

Club shop: At the ground; stocks all types of souvenirs.

Handbooks/programmes: Programmes available on subscription.

Club Colours: Blue shirts, white shorts, royal blue stockings, white tops.

Change Colours: Red shirts, white shorts, red and white stockings.

Club Nickname: 'Blues' or 'Spireites'.

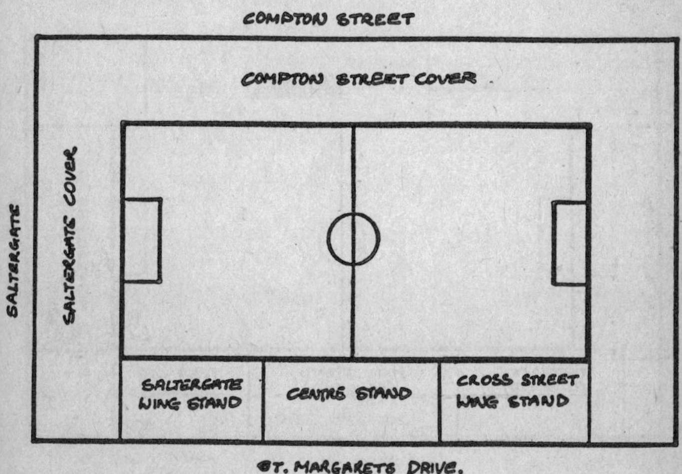

COLCHESTER UNITED

LAYER RD. GROUND, COLCHESTER.

TELEPHONE 74042.

Telegraphic Address: 'United Colchester'.

Ground capacity: 16.150. **Pitch measurements:** 110 yds × 73 yds.

How to get there: Buses from Butt Road in Colchester, which is about 2 miles from the railway station. Also buses from town centre and bus station.

Match tickets: Stand seats can be booked 2 weeks in advance (Ticket Office tel: Colchester 72202).

Car parking: Parking facilities in Butt Road and Layer Road, approximately 150 yards past the ground on the south side of Colchester. Free parking in army barracks (150 yards).

Entertainments/catering facilities: Refreshment points on the ground.

Club shop: Sells all types of souvenirs; mailing list on request.

Handbooks/programmes: Back numbers of programmes can be ordered from the club shop.

Club Colours: Blue and white vertical stripes, blue shorts, white stockings.

Change Colours: All red.

Club Nickname: 'The U's'.

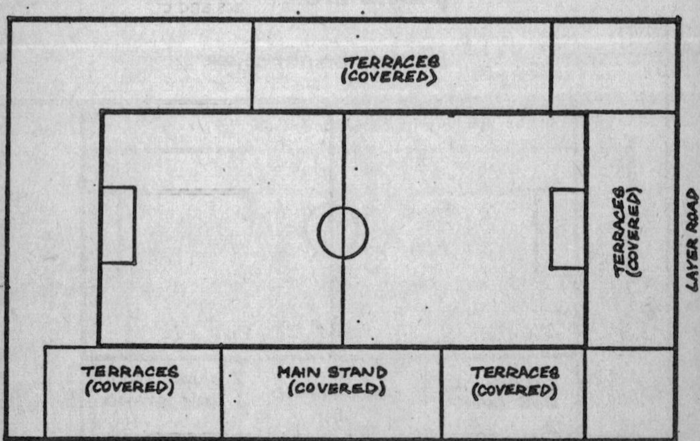

COVENTRY CITY

HIGHFIELD RD., COVENTRY.

TELEPHONE COVENTRY 57171.

Telegraphic address: 'City Football Coventry'.

Ground capacity: 47,000 (16,000 covered). **Pitch measurements:** 110 yds × 75 yds.

How to get there: Buses from Coventry railway station to town centre (Pool Meadow bus station). Then buses 1, 4, 7, 8, 8A to ground.

Match tickets: Stand seat tickets can be booked 28 days in advance of any home League fixture. Postal applications accepted if sent with correct remittance.

Car parking: Street parking permitted all around the ground.

Entertainments/catering facilities: Pre-match entertainment at all League and Cup games by Radio Sky Blue; live entertainment from groups and bands at special matches. The Sky Blue Buttery is open for hot and cold snacks before matches. There are 16 licensed refreshment rooms and lounges, and 11 unlicensed refreshment rooms and lounges around the ground; all are open before the game, at half-time, and after the match. The Grandstand restaurant, recommended by Egon Ronay, is open for lunch Mon. to Fri. and Is availabie in the evening for private dinner parties.

Club shop: Sited in the main stand; sells all types of souvenirs.

Handbooks/programmes: Programmes available through a postal service.

Extra information: Coventry City Supporters' Club under the Thackhall St. Stand welcome visiting supporters on production of the membership card of their own club.

Club Colours: Sky blue shirts, navy and white facings, sky blue shorts, sky blue stockings.

Change Colours: Cherry red shirts, royal blue collars and cuffs, blue shorts, red stockings.

Club Nickname: 'Sky Blues'.

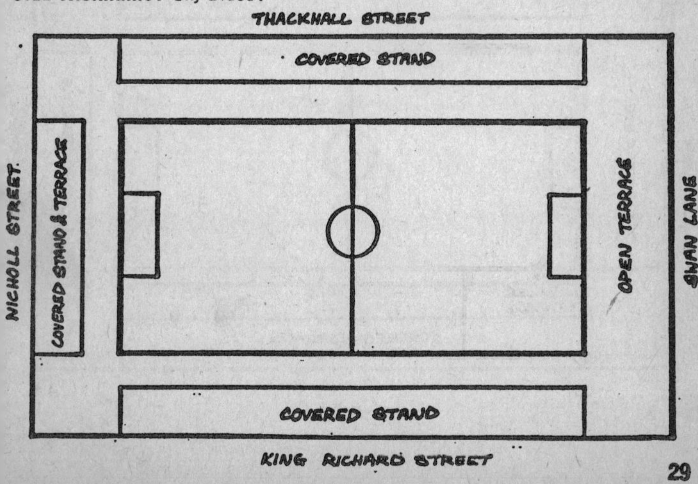

CREWE ALEXANDRA

FOOTBALL GROUND, GRESTY RD., CREWE.

TELEPHONE CREWE 3014.

Telegraphic address: 'Alex Football Crewe'.

Ground capacity: 17,000. **Pitch measurements:** 113 yds × 75 yds. **Address of Supporters Club:** Registered Office, Crewe Alexandra, Supporters Association, 131 Edleston Road, Crewe, Cheshire.

How to get there: Local bus services from outlying districts. The ground is situated just five minutes' walk from Crewe railway station.

Match tickets: Advance booking for important cup ties only.

Car parking: Parking at the ground for 120 cars.

Entertainments/catering facilities: The Alexandra Club adjoining the ground is owned by the club. Refreshment points inside the ground.

Club shop: Situated at the ground; sells all types of souvenirs.

Handbooks/programmes: Handbooks on sale at matches.

Club Colours: Red shirts, red shorts, red stockings.

Change Colours: White shirts, black shorts, white stockings.

Club Nickname: 'The Railwaymen'.

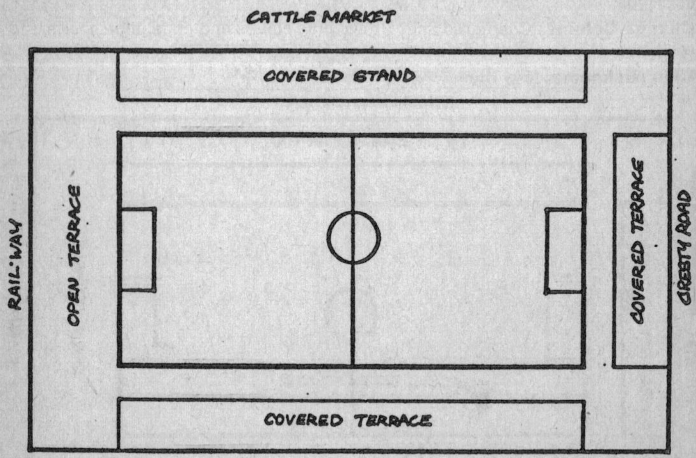

CRYSTAL PALACE

SELHURST PARK, LONDON, SE25 6PU.

TELEPHONE 01-653-2223/4.

Ground capacity: 51,000 (21,000 covered). **Pitch measurements:** 110 yds × 75 yds.

How to get there: Ground served by three stations—Selhurst (5 minutes walk), Norwood Junction (7 minutes) and Thornton Heath (10 minutes). Buses 68, 75, 154, 157, 12 (to Norwood Junction).

Match tickets: Seats bookable in advance in Old Stand; postal applications accepted one month in advance and personal application two weeks in advance. Postal applications must be accompanied by S.A.E. and the correct remittance. Cheques must be made payable to Crystal Palace F.C. and name and address must be written on the back. Separate application must be made for each match.

Car parking: Large car park at the ground.

Entertainments/catering facilities: A social hall and catering facilities within the ground.

Club shops: Two shops sell all types of souvenirs.

Handbooks/programmes: Programmes available on subscription.

Club Colours: Royal blue and red vertical striped shirts, royal blue shorts, royal blue stockings with red and white bands.

Change Colours: All white.

Club Nickname: 'The Eagles'.

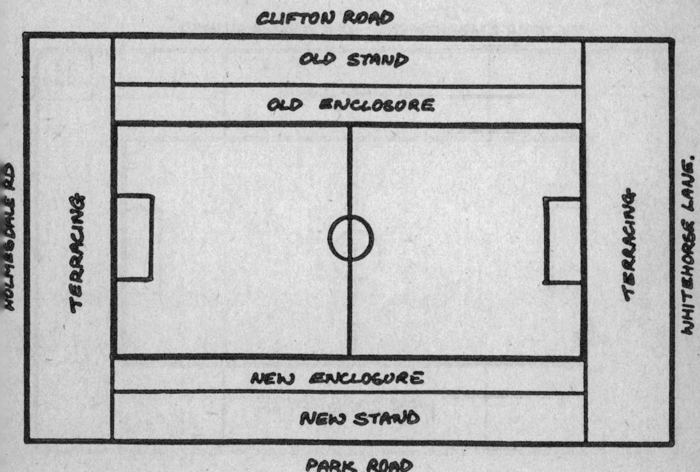

DARLINGTON

FEETHAMS GROUND, DARLINGTON.

TELEPHONE DARLINGTON 65097/67712.

Ground capacity: 20,000. **Pitch measurements:** 110 yds × 74 yds. **Address of Supporters Club:** Same as Football Club.

How to get there: Darlington railway station, five minutes walk.

Match tickets: Postal and telephone bookings accepted in advance of the match.

Car parking: Ample parking in surrounding side-streets.

Entertainments/catering facilities: Four nearby cafés. Three snack bars in the ground.

Club shop: Shops inside the ground sell all types of souvenirs.

Handbooks/programmes: No handbook. Programmes available on subscription.

Extra information: The club will make every effort to cater for the disabled, the blind, or any person who has some difficulty seeking entrance because of illness.

Club Colours: White shirts, white shorts, white stockings.

Club Nickname: 'The Quakers'.

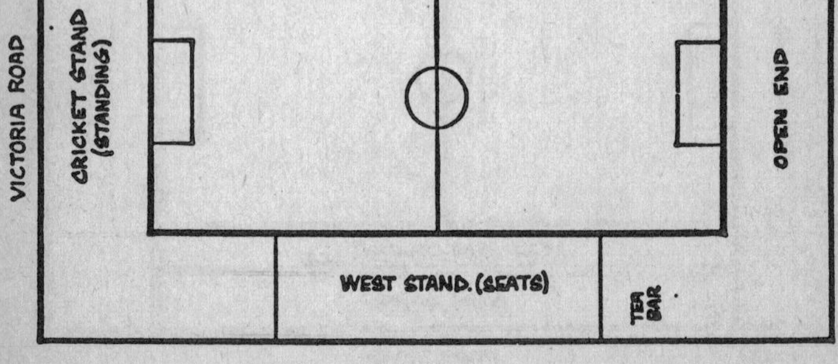

DERBY COUNTY

BASEBALL GROUND, SHAFTESBURY CRESCENT, DERBY DE3 8NB.
TELEPHONE DERBY 40105.

Telegraphic Address: 'Football Derby'.

Ground capacity: 39,500 (38,000 covered, 12,250 seats.) **Pitch measurements:** 110 yds × 71 yds. **Address of Supporters Club:** Baseball Ground, Derby.

How to get there: Buses from town centre 60, 88 and 99. Nearest railway station Derby Midland.

Match tickets: Available 2 weeks in advance, £1.50, £1.20, £1.00.

Car parking: Eight car parks within half a mile of the ground run by the club in connection with the local corporation. Street parking half a mile from the ground.

Entertainments/catering facilities: Sportsman Club (members only). Licensed and refreshment bars in all parts of the ground.

Club shop: The Ramtique in Osmaston Road open every week day. Shop on the ground open on match days.

Handbooks/programmes: Yearbook published annually. "The Ram", the club newspaper and official programme, available on subscription c/o The Programme Editor, Derby County F.C.

Club Colours: White shirts, blue shorts, white stockings.

Change Colours: Blue shirts, white shorts, blue stockings.

Club Nickname: 'The Rams'.

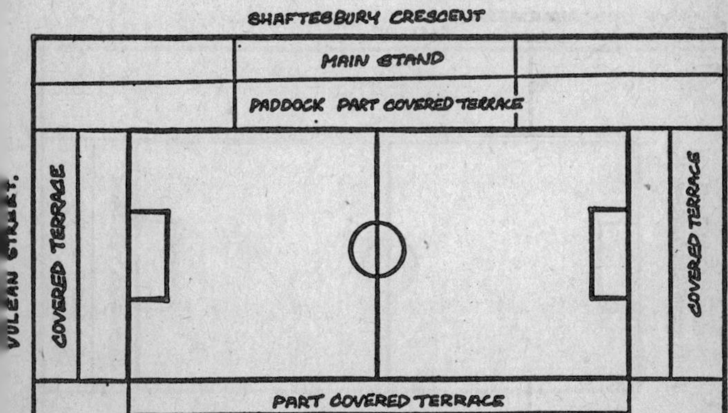

DONCASTER ROVERS

BELLE VUE GROUND, DONCASTER.

TELEPHONE DONCASTER 55281.

Telegraphic Address: 'Rovers Doncaster'.

Ground capacity: 30,000. **Pitch measurements:** 118 yds × 79 yrds. **Address of Supporters Club:** Secretary, K. J. Avis, 64 Harrowden Road, Doncaster.

How to get there: Buses from town centre (Duke St.)—Race Course, Hyde Park, and Cantley Estate services. Doncaster railway station is near the town centre.

Match tickets: No advance booking except for Cup ties.

Car parking: Very large car and coach park adjoining the ground. Entrance direct from Great North Road.

Entertainments/catering facilities: Refreshment bars in Main Stand and around the ground, including licensed bars. No entertainments but a social club adjoins the ground.

Club shop: In Main Stand, stocks all types of souvenirs.

Handbooks/programmes: Annual handbook on sale at 20p post free or at shop or Supporters Club office. Programmes on sale at shop but not on subscription.

Club Colours: White shirts with two red hoops, red shorts and white stockings.

Change Colours: Red shirts with white facings, white shorts with red stripe, white stockings.

Club Nickname: 'Rovers'.

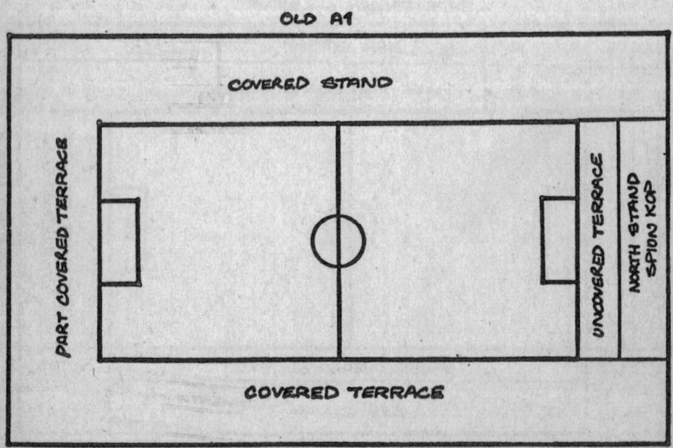

EVERTON

GOODISON PARK, LIVERPOOL L4 4EL.

TELEPHONE 051-525-5263/4.

Ground capacity: 58,000. (25,000 seats.) **Pitch measurements:** 112 yds × 78 yds.
Address of Supporters Club: 38 City Rd., Liverpool 4.

How to get there: Corporation buses 19 and 44 from Pierhead, 68 from Old Swan 3, 22, 25, 500 from South End of the City and 30, 92, 92a, 92b, 93 from City centre. Nearest railway station, Liverpool Lime Street.

Match tickets: Reserved stand seats are available for all home fixtures (except the match v Liverpool) at any time during the season, either by post or by personal application to the Box Office at the Bullens Rd. side of the ground (tel: 051-525-0080). The Box Office is open each weekday from 9 a.m. to 5 p.m. Postal applications should be addressed to the Box Office manager and contain the correct remittance and S.A.E.

Car parking: Extensive parking facilities on site at the corner of Priory Rd. and Utting Ave.

Entertainments/catering facilities: Royal Blue Social Club offers cabaret entertainment each Saturday and Sunday; visiting parties by arrangement. Royal Blue Restaurant open to the public for lunch on Mondays to Fridays but restricted to members on match days.

Club shop: All souvenirs available from The Toffee Shops in Goodison Rd. and Bullens Rd.; send S.A.E. for mail order list.

Handbooks/programmes: Match-day magazine available on seasonal subscription.

Club Colours: Blue shirts with white collars, white shorts and stockings.

Change Colours: Amber shirts, royal blue shorts.

Club Nickname: 'Toffeemen' or 'Blues'

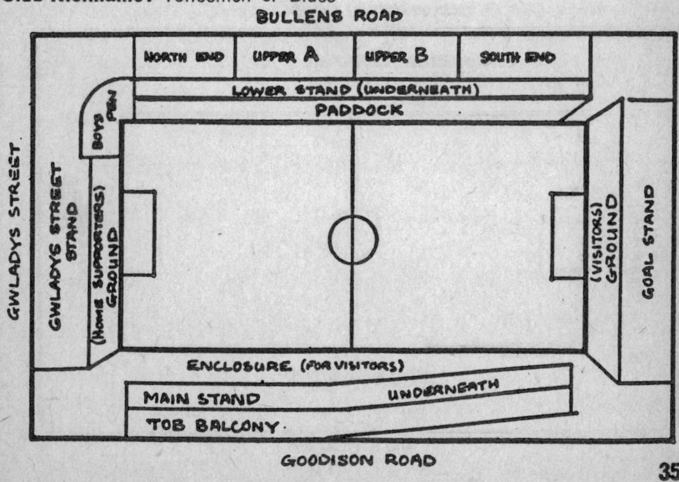

EXETER CITY

ST. JAMES PARK, EXETER.

TELEPHONE EXETER 54073.

Ground capacity: 18,500. **Pitch measurements:** 114 yds × 73 yds. **Address of Supporters Club:** Same as Football Club.

How to get there: City buses A, D, J, K. S from city centre to The Fountain (one-minute walk to the ground). Routes G and S pass both railway stations—Exeter St. Davids and Exeter Central.

Match tickets: Tickets may be booked in advance usually two weeks before home matches.

Car parking: No car park at the ground. Limited streei parking permitted.

Entertainments/catering facilities: A members social club is situated at the ground. Subscription £1.00; joint membership £1.50.

Club shop: Sells all types of souvenirs.

Handbooks/programmes: Handbooks available at 20p; programmes can be ordered on subscription.

Club Colours: Red and white striped shirts, red shorts, red and white stockings.

Change Colours: Blue and white striped shirts, blue shorts, blue and white stockings.

Club Nickname: 'The Grecians'.

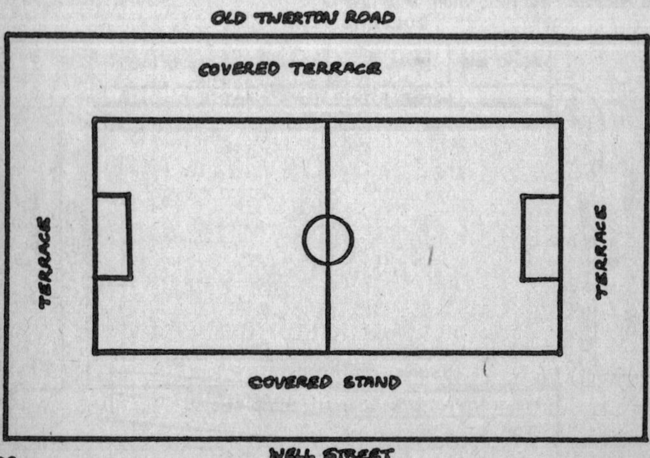

FULHAM

CRAVEN COTTAGE, STEVENAGE RD., FULHAM, LONDON S.W.6.

TELEPHONE 01-736-5621/7035.

POOLS OFFICE: 736 4634.

Telegraphic Address: 'Fulhamish, London, S.W.6.'

Ground capacity: 42,000. **Pitch measurements:** 110 yds × 75 yds. **Address of Supporters Club:** Fulham Travel Club, Craven Cottage, Stevenage Road, S.W.6.

How to get there: Underground stations, Putney Bridge (District Line) and Hammersmith (District, Metropolitan, Piccadilly). Then by bus—30, 74, 85, 93, 220.

Match tickets: The Box Office is linked up by computer to Seat Reservation Systems and Keith Prowse. Seats can be reserved for any home game during the season.

Car parking: Plentiful parking in streets around the ground.

Entertainments/catering facilities: Social amenities available. Snack bars and licensed bars around the ground.

Club shop: Sells all types of souvenirs.

Handbooks/programmes: Both handbooks and programmes available.

Club Colours: White shirts, black shorts with two white stripes, white stockings.

Change Colours: Yellow shirts, blue shorts, yellow stockings.

Club Nickname: 'Cottagers'.

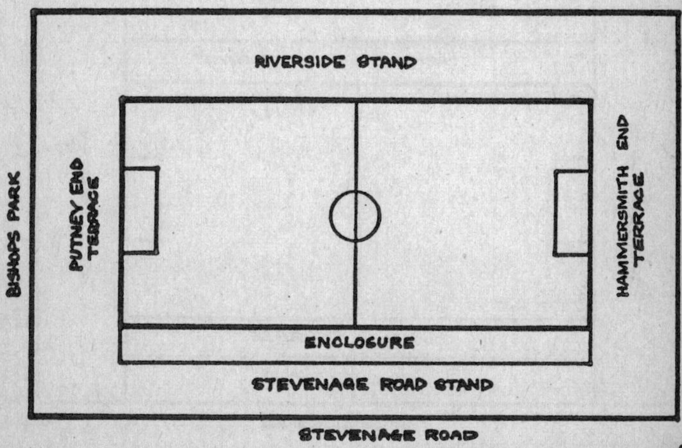

GILLINGHAM

PRIESTFIELD STADIUM, GILLINGHAM.

TELEPHONE MEDWAY 51854.

Telegraphic Address: 'Football, Gillingham, Kent'.

Ground capacity: 22,000. **Pitch measurements:** 114 yds × 75 yds. **Address of Supporters Club:** Gillingham F.C. Supporters' Association, Gordon Road, Gillingham.

How to get there: Gillingham railway station (six or seven minutes' walk). Bus services are 10 minutes from ground.

Match tickets: Can be reserved by postal application enclosing correct remittance and S.A.E.

Car parking: Park for 500 cars adjoining the ground, entrance in Toronto Rd.

Entertainments/catering facilities: A club house, and several bars around the ground.

Club shop: Sells all types of souvenirs.

Handbooks/programmes: Programmes available on subscription. Handbooks also available.

Club Colours: Blue shirts, white shorts, blue stockings, white and blue trim.

Change Colours: Amber shirts, black shorts, black stockings.

Club Nickname: 'The Gills'.

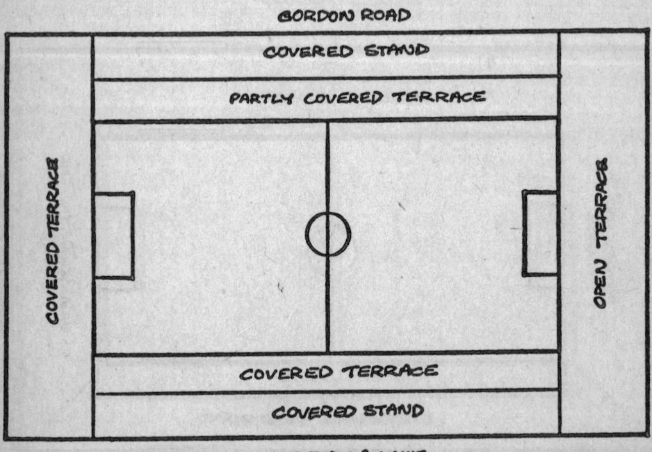

GRIMSBY TOWN

BLUNDELL PARK, CLEETHORPES, LINCOLNSHIRE.

TELEPHONE CLEETHORPES 61420 and 61803.

Telegraphic address: 'Football Grimsby'.

Ground capacity: 28,000. **Pitch measurements:** 111 yds × 74 yds. **Address of Club Shop:** Junior Club Souvenir Shop, Blundell Park, Cleethorpes.

How to get there: Buses 3, 3A, 3F, 9 run to the ground; also football specials from the town centre. Nearest railway stations are Cleethorpes and Grimsby Town.

Match tickets: Seating can be booked one month in advance.

Car parking: Parking permitted in all side streets around the ground.

Entertainments/catering facilities: A licensed bar and several snack bars.

Club shop: There are 3 club shops, run by the Grimsby Town Junior Club, selling all types of souvenirs.

Handbooks/programmes: Programmes: on sale at matches.

Club Colours: Black and white striped shirts, black shorts, red stockings.

Change Colours: All white.

Club Nickname: 'The Mariners'.

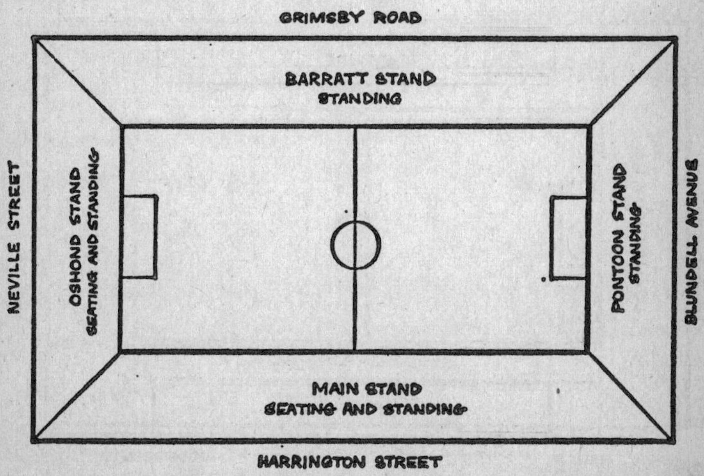

HALIFAX TOWN

SHAY GROUND, HALIFAX.

TELEPHONE HALIFAX 53423.

Ground capacity: 25,000. **Pitch measurements:** 110 yds × 70 yds. **Address of Supporters Club:** Same as Football Club.

How to get there: Near the town centre within a few minutes walking distance of the bus station and railway station.

Match tickets: Advance booking on application to the secretary.

Car parking: Car park is available; entrance in Shaw Hill.

Entertainments/catering facilities: Social club adjacent to the club office. Catering facilities at points inside the ground.

Club shop: Sells all types of souvenirs.

Handbooks/programmes: Handbooks and programmes available from Supporters Club, c.o Halifax Town A.F.C.

Club Colours: Royal blue shirts with amber collar and numbers, royal blue shorts, amber stripe, blue stockings.

Change colours: Green and black striped shirts, black shorts, black stockings.

Club Nickname: 'Town'.

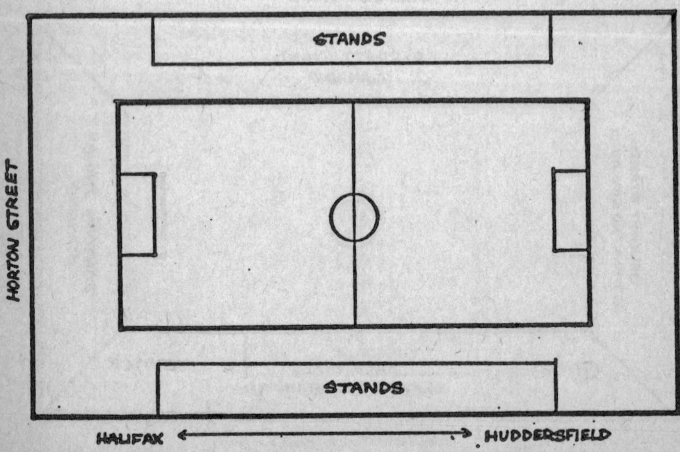

HARTLEPOOL

THE VICTORIA GROUND.

TELEPHONE HARTLEPOOL 2584.
18 SCARBOROUGH STREET, HARTLEPOOL. TELEPHONE 3492 (Office).

Ground capacity: 19,500. **Pitch measurements:** 113 yds × 77 yds.

How to get there: Hartlepool railway station is only a few hundred yards from the ground. Local bus services run scheduled services to Hartlepool.

Match tickets: No pre-booking of tickets.

Car parking: Ample side-street parking.

Entertainments/catering facilities: Two refreshment kiosks inside the ground.

Club shop: Open on match days; stocks all types of souvenirs.

Handbooks/programmes: No handbooks. Programmes available on subscription.

Club Colours: Blue shirts, white shorts, blue and white stockings.

Change Colour: Red shirts, black shorts, blue and white stockings.

Club Nickname: 'The Pool'.

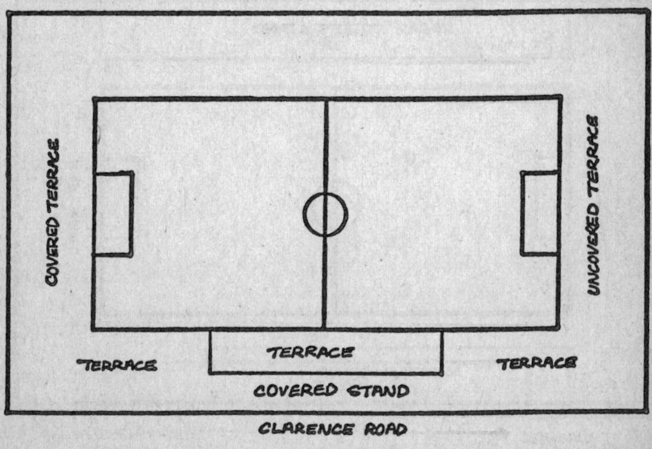

HEREFORD UNITED

EDGAR STREET, HEREFORD.

TELEPHONE HEREFORD (0432) 4037.

Ground capacity: 17,500. **Pitch measurements:** 111 yds × 80 yds.

How to get there: Ground very close to town centre, within five minutes walking distance from Hereford railway station and the bus station.

Match tickets: Tickets can be booked in advance.

Car parking: Parking is available around the ground for approximately 1,000 vehicles.

Entertainments/catering facilities: Canteens on the ground. A social club is in the process of construction.

Club shop: All types of souvenirs sold.

Handbooks/programmes: Programmes available on application to the club shop.

Club Colours: White shirts, black shorts, black and white stockings.

Change Colours: Yellow, blue, yellow.

Club Nickname: 'United'.

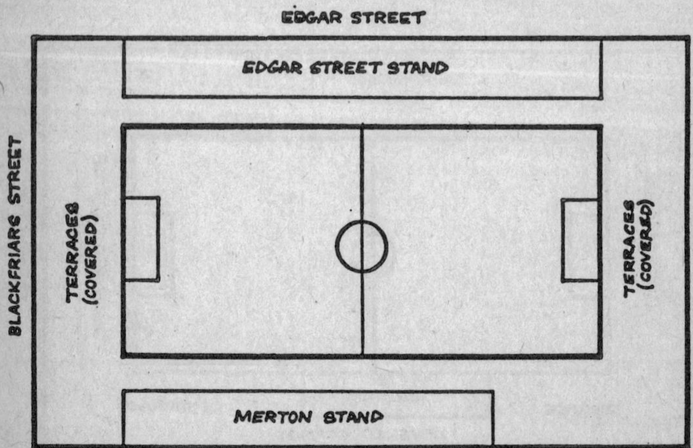

HUDDERSFIELD TOWN

LEEDS RD., HUDDERSFIELD.

TELEPHONE HUDDERSFIELD 20335/6.

Ground capacity: 48,000. **Pitch measurements:** 115 yds × 75 yds. **Address of Supporters Club:** Supporters Club Offices, 286 Leeds Road, Huddersfield, Yorkshire.

How to get there: The ground is one mile from the town centre via Corporation buses 40, 41, 42. On match days special buses run from the centre. By road, the ground can be reached along Leeds Road either from the town centre or from Leeds.

Match tickets: Admission to all parts is by payment at the turnstiles except for special matches. (tel: Huddersfield 36100).

Car parking: Ample parking accommodation on all four sides of the ground; in the region of 6,000 cars can be parked within 200 yards of the turnstiles.

Entertainments/catering facilities: No social club, but there are 11 unlicensed snack bars around the ground.

Club shop: Close to the ground; sells all types of souvenirs (tel: Huddersfield 31028).

Handbooks/programmes: Programmes available on subscription from the club shop.

Club Colours: Blue and white striped shirts, white shorts and stockings.

Change Colours: Yellow shirts, green shorts, yellow stockings.

Club Nickname: 'The Terriers'.

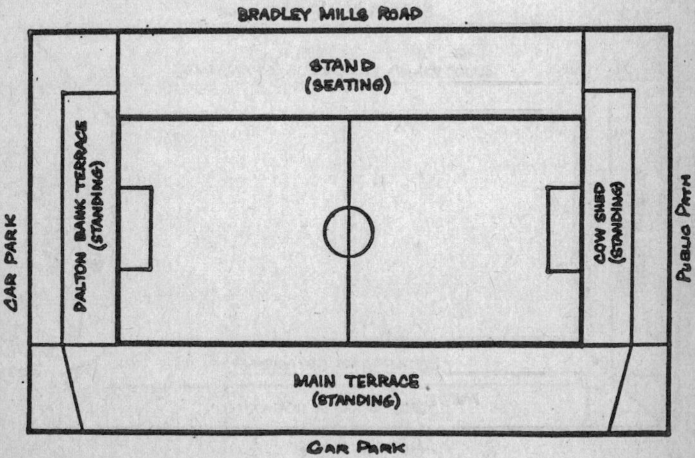

HULL CITY

BOOTHFERRY PARK, HULL HU4 6EU.

TELEPHONE 0482 52195/6/7.

Telegraphic address: 'Tigers Hull'.

Ground capacity: 42,000. **Pitch measurements:** 112 yds × 75 yds.

How to get there: Buses 55, 57, 43, 48 from coach station, Ferensway, Hull. Nearest railway stations, Hull Paragon and Boothferry Park Halt. Special trains on match days from Hull Paragon to Boothferry Park Halt; admittance to ground through turnstiles on station. Ground situated on A63 to the west of the city.

Match tickets: Tickets for League games may be booked two weeks in advance of the match.

Car parking: Official car park at ground for season passholders only. Public car park, Kempton Road park two minutes walk away; coach park in Pickering Road five minutes from ground

Entertainments/catering facilities: Catering facilities at points around the ground.

Club shop: In the South Stand and open on League match days.

Handbooks/programmes: Programmes available on subscription.

Club Colours: Amber shirts with black collars and cuffs, black shorts, black stockings.

Change Colours: All white.

Club Nickname: 'Tigers'.

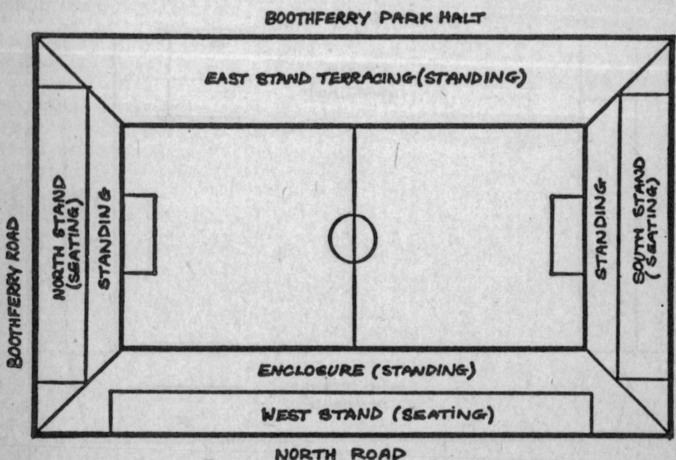

IPSWICH TOWN

PORTMAN RD., IPSWICH, SUFFOLK.

TELEPHONE: IPSWICH 51306 and 57107.

Ground capacity: 36,000. **Pitch measurements:** 112 yds × 75 yds. **Address of Supporters Club:** Same as Football Club.

How to get there: The ground is central and only two minutes walk from Ipswich railway station; the town centre is five minutes away. Local buses run past the ground.

Match tickets: Seats bookable 12 days before the match.

Car parking: Large parks in Portman Road, Portman's Walk, and off Princes Street at Greyfriars Park.

Entertainments/catering facilities: Restaurant in Portman Road. Tea bars around the ground.

Club shops: Four on the ground stock all types of souvenirs.

Handbooks/programmes: Programmes available on subscription.

Club Colours: Blue shirts, white shorts, and blue stockings.

Change Colours: Yellow shirts, blue shorts, yellow stockings.

Club Nickname: 'Town' or 'blues'.

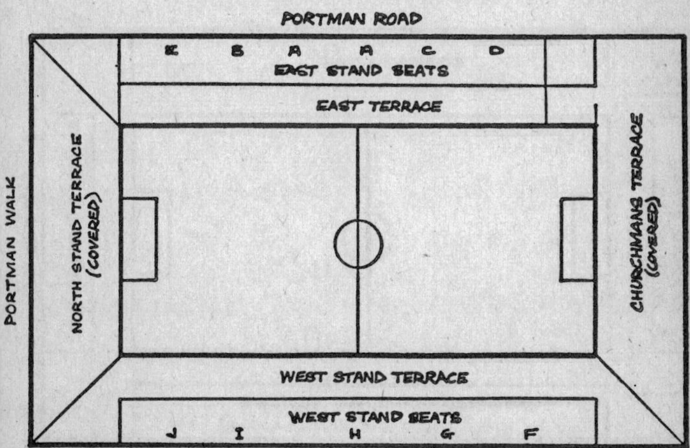

LEEDS UNITED

ELLAND RD., LEEDS 11.
TELEPHONE LEEDS 716037/8.

Telegraphic Address: 'Football Leeds'.

Ground capacity: 50,000. **Pitch measurements:** 117 × 76 yds. **Address of Supporters Club:** Leeds United Supporters Club, Fullerton Park, Elland Road, Leeds 11.

How to get there: Nearest railway station, Leeds City. The city centre is within walking distance from the station and then by Corporation buses to the ground.

Match tickets: Tickets are available for advance sale. The number will depend on demand for season tickets.

Car parking: Within one minute of the ground there is a large park owned by the Leeds Greyhound Association; this holds about 1,000 cars. Street parking in the immediate vicinity. Large park on the Beeston Ring Road.

Entertainments/catering facilities: Supporters' social club adjacent to the ground. Snack bars around the ground.

Club shop: This operates at the ground next to the Pools Office and stocks all types of souvenirs.

Handbooks/programmes: Both handbooks and programmes are available from the club shop; programmes are available on subscription.

Club Colours: All white.

Change Colours: All yellow.

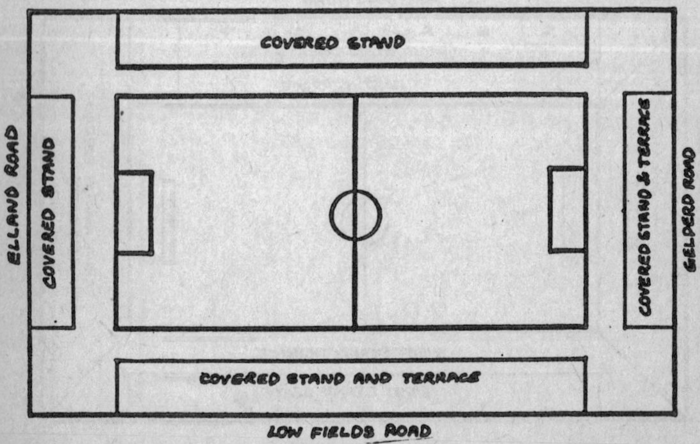

LEICESTER CITY

FILBERT ST., LEICESTER.

TELEPHONE LEICESTER 57111/2 (MATCH INFORMATION LEICESTER 539199).

Pitch measurements: 112 yds × 75 yds.

How to get there: Corporation buses from Humberstone Gate and Waterloo St. (opposite railway station) in city centre. Nearest station Leicester London Road. Midland Red run bus services to the town centre from outlying districts.

Match tickets: Seats can be booked from two matches in advance.

Car parking: Parking adjacent to the ground is for season-ticket holders only. There is nearby street parking and also a public car park about five minutes walk from the ground.

Entertainments/catering facilities: A private season-ticket members bar in the main stand, and catering bars in all sections of the ground.

Club shop: Situated under the main stand; sells all types of souvenirs.

Handbooks/programmes: Both handbooks and programmes are available from the club shop.

Club Colours: Blue shirts with white collar and cuffs, white shorts, white stockings.

Change Colours: Red shirts, white shorts, navy stockings.

Club Nickname: 'Filberts' and 'Foxes'.

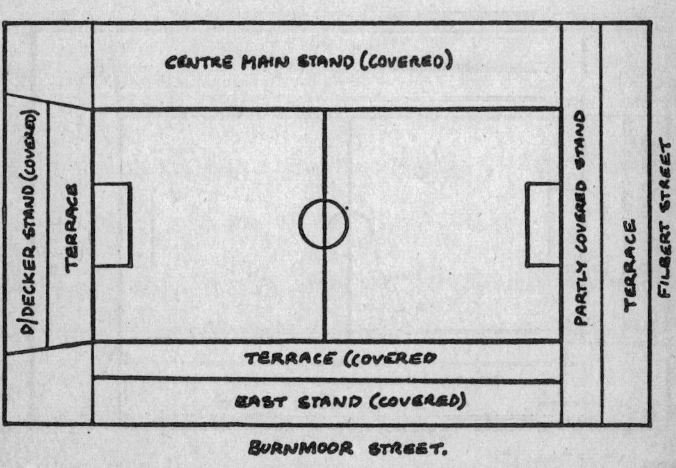

LINCOLN CITY

SINCIL BANK, LINCOLN.

TELEPHONE LINCOLN 21912 AND 21298.

Ground capacity: 25,300. **Pitch measurements:** 110 yds × 75 yds.

How to get there: There is a regular bus service from Lincoln Central Station to the ground, although there are no special buses. Nearest stations are Lincoln Central and Lincoln St Marks.

Match tickets: Bookings accepted by telephone or by letter. They are received up to 5.00 p.m. on the Friday before a Saturday match and up to 5.00 p.m. on the Tuesday before a Wednesday night match.

Car parking: Limited to 150 cars at the ground.

Entertainments/catering facilities: Social club at the ground with light catering before and after the match.

Club shop: Sited on the ground; sells all types of souvenirs.

Handbooks/programmes: Programmes available at each game or by subscription.

Club Colours: Red and white striped shirts, black shorts, red and white stockings.

Change Colours: Yellow shirts, blue shorts, yellow stockings.

Club Nickname: 'The Red Imps'.

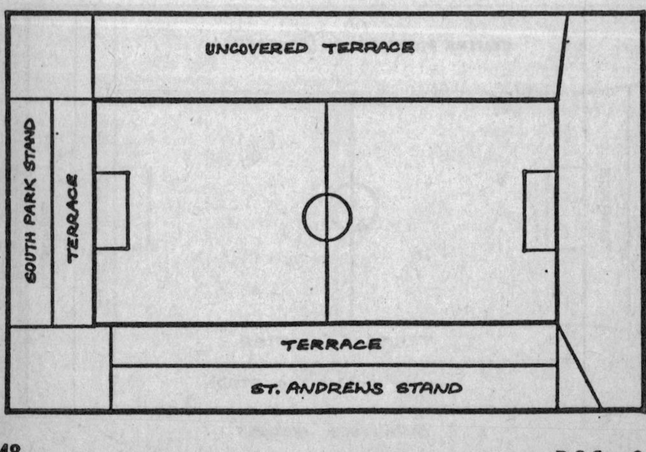

 R.C.G.—2

LIVERPOOL

ANFIELD ROAD, LIVERPOOL 4.
TELEPHONE 051-263-2361.

Telegraphic address: 'Goalkeeper Liverpool'.

Ground capacity: 56,318. **Pitch measurements:** 110 yds × 75 yds. **Address of Supporters Club:** 1 Lower Breck Rd.

How to get there: Buses 17d from Pier Head and 26, 27 from Castle Street. Nearest stations, Bankhall and Kirkdale.

Match tickets: Postal applications 19 days before the match.

Car parking: Limited street parking around the ground. Large privately owned car park in Priory Road within five minutes walk of the ground.

Entertainments/catering facilities: Licensed refreshment bars in all parts of the ground.

Club shop: Main shop run by the Development Association open Monday–Saturday. Small kiosks in the ground open on match days only.

Handbooks/programmes: No handbook. Programmes available on subscription from the secretary.

Club Colours: All red with white facings.

Change Colours: White shirts with red collars and cuffs, black shorts, white stockings.

Club Nickname: 'Reds' or 'Pool'.

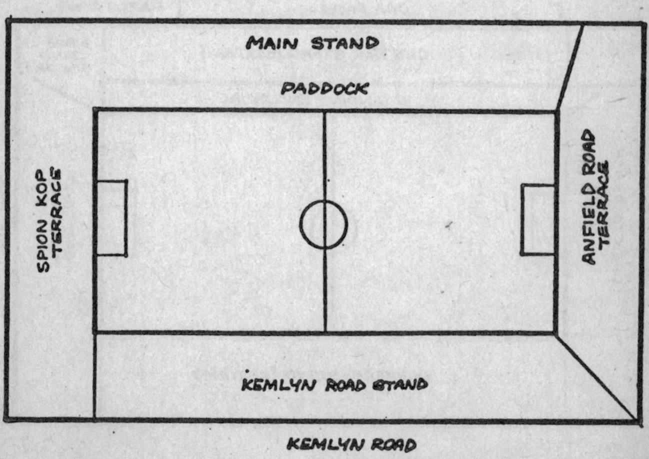

LUTON TOWN

70–72 KENILWORTH RD., LUTON.

TELEPHONE LUTON 23151–2.

Telegraphic Address: 'Football, Luton'.

Ground capacity: 25,000 (17,000 covered). **Pitch measurements:** 112 yds × 72 yds.

How to get there: Nearest railway station, Luton Midland (six minutes walk). There is also a frequent bus service to and from the town centre to the ground, but the ground is central.

Match tickets: Seats can be booked one month before the game.

Car parking: Ample parking facilities adjacent to the ground entrance in Maple Road.

Entertainments/catering facilities: Licensed bars and refreshment bars on ground.

Club shop: Sells all types of souvenirs.

Handbooks/programmes: Handbooks and programmes can be obtained from club shop.

Club Colours: Orange shirt with one navy and one white vertical stripe on left side. Navy blue shorts. Orange stockings.

Change Colours: White shirts, navy shorts, white stockings.

Club Nickname: 'Hatters'.

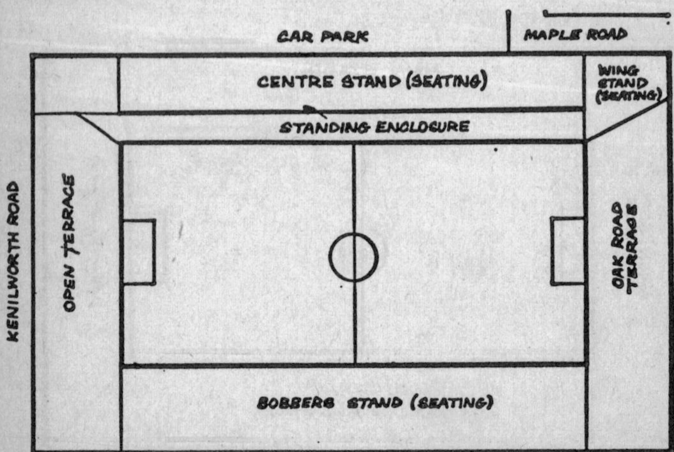

MANCHESTER CITY

MAINE ROAD, MOSS SIDE, MANCHESTER 4.

TELEPHONE 061-226-1191/2.

Telegraphic Address: 'Football, Manchester 14'.

Capacity crowd: 52,500. **Pitch measurements:** 117 yds × 79 yds.

How to get there: Corporation specials from Aytoun Street, Piccadilly, in centre of city. Nearest railway station, Manchester Piccadilly.

Match tickets: Advance booking 14 days prior to the match.

Car parking: Kippax Street car park holds approximately 400 cars. Also street parking.

Entertainments/catering facilities: Social club can be used by visiting supporters (contact Mr Roy Clarke). Licensed refreshment points around the ground.

Club shop: Open all week at the ground.

Handbook/programmes: Handbook available. Programmes can be obtained on a mailing list.

Club Colours: Sky blue shirts with white collars and cuffs, white shorts, blue stockings.

Change Colours: Red and black striped shirts, black shorts.

Club Nickname: 'Citizens'.

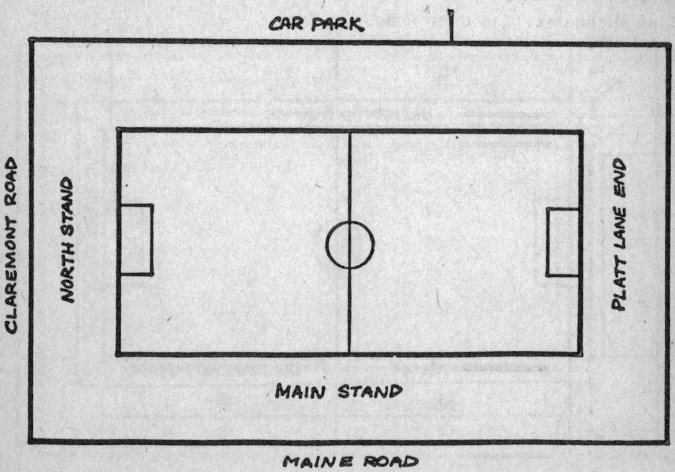

MANCHESTER UNITED

OLD TRAFFORD, MANCHESTER M16 0RA.

TELEPHONE 061-872-1661/2.

Telegraphic Address: 'Stadium Manchester'.

Ground capacity: 61,500 **Pitch measurements:** 116 yds × 76 yds.

How to get there: Special buses from Aytoun Street, Cannon Street, and various points in Manchester and Salford. Frequent train service from Manchester Oxford Road station direct to the Football Ground station, returning after the match. Schedule services from Oxford Road and Knott Mill, Manchester, or from Altrincham, Timperley, and intermediate stations run to Warwick Road station, only a few minutes walk from the ground.

Match tickets: Seats can be booked from two calendar months before the match. Any not sold by Monday before a Saturday match can be reserved by personal appliation. For up-to-date ticket information, tel.: 061-872 7771.

Car parking: Large car parks within easy reach of the ground at Chester Road municipal park (1,000 cars), Lancashire County Cricket Ground, Talbot Road and Great Stone Road (1,200), White City Stadium, Chester Road (900), British Car Auctions, Talbot Road (100), and the former Deaf and Dumb School, entrance Talbot Road/Boyer Street (300).

Entertainments/catering facilities: Licensed bars around the ground.

Club shop: Souvenir shop alongside the ticket office.

Handbooks/programmes: Not available on subscription but application with remittance can be sent to the ground for individual matches.

Club Colours: Red shirts with white collars and cuffs, white shorts, black stockings with red tops and white band.

Change Colours: All white.

Club Nickname: 'United', or 'Reds'.

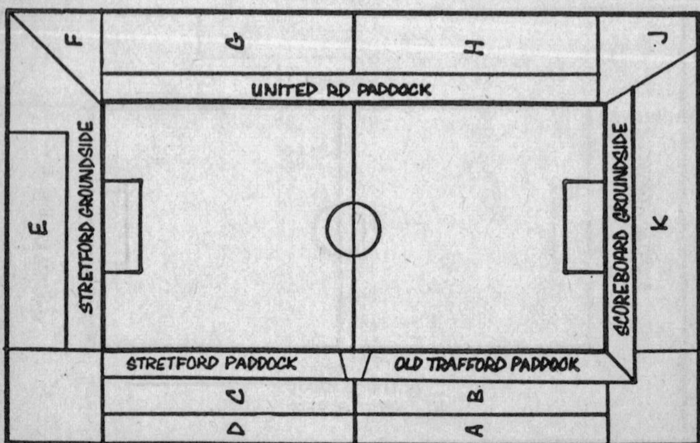

MANSFIELD TOWN

FIELD MILL GROUND, QUARRY LANE, MANSFIELD.
TELEPHONE MANSFIELD 23567.

Telegraphic Address: 'Football, Mansfield'.

Capacity crowd: 23,500. **Pitch measurements:** 115 yds × 72 yds. **Address of Supporters Club:** Jackpot Office, c/o the ground.

How to get there: Buses from town centre to within 300 yards of the ground. Nearest railway station, Alfreton and Mansfield Parkway.

Match tickets: Advance booking 5 days prior to match.

Car parking: Room for 500 cars at the ground and anolher 3,000 within 500 yards.

Entertainments/catering facilities: No Club room. Licensed tea bars in the ground.

Club shop: Adjacent to the ground: sells all types of souvenirs.

Handbooks/programmes: Both on sale at the club shop.

Club Colours: Amber shirts, blue shorts, amber stockings.

Change Colours: White shirts with blue and amber trimmings, blue shorts, white stockings.

Club Nickname: 'The Stags'.

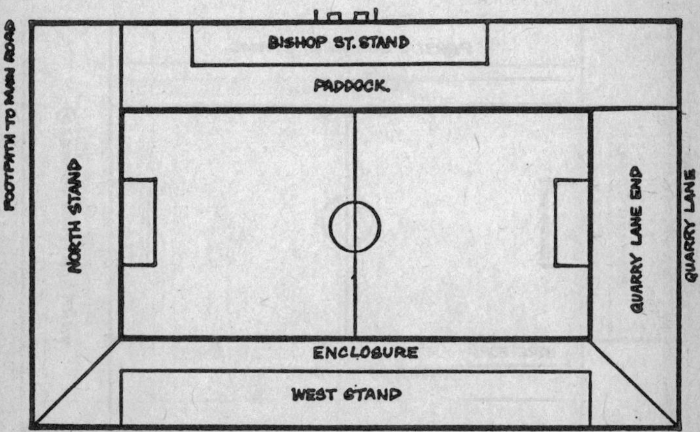

MIDDLESBROUGH

AYRESOME PARK, MIDDLESBROUGH, TEESIDE.
TELEPHONE MIDDLESBROUGH 89659/85996.

Telegraphic Address: 'Football, Middlesbrough'.

Ground capacity: 42,000. **Pitch measurements:** 115 yds × 75 yds.

How to get there: Regular buses from the Exchange in Middlesbrough to the ground. Buses also from bus station next to Middlesbrough railway station.

Match tickets: By postal or personal application two weeks prior to the match.

Car parking: Off-street parking near the ground.

Entertainments/catering facilities: Social club (members only); refreshment bars around the ground.

Handbooks/programmes: Programmes available on subscription.

Club Colours: Red shirts with 2in. wide white band round chest, red shorts with white stripe down sides, red stockings with white tops.

Change Colours: Black and royal blue vertical striped shirts, black shorts and stockings.

Club Nickname: 'The Boro'.

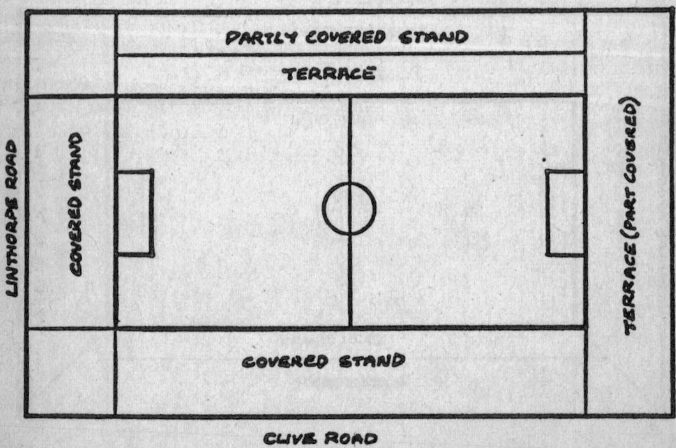

MILLWALL

THE DEN, COLD BLOW LANE, LONDON, S.E.14.

TELEPHONE 01-639 3143/4.

Ground capacity: 40,000. **Pitch measurements:** 112 yds × 74 yds. **Address of Supporters Club:** Same as Ground.

How to get there: Buses from Central London and West End: 36, 36A, 36B, 53, 141, 163, 171, 177, 182 From City: 21. Nearest Underground stations, New Cross or New Cross Gate (Metropolitan Line). Also New Cross Gate British Rail station.

Match tickets: Bookable 10–14 days in advance.

Car parking: N.C.P. car park near the ground. Also ample street parking.

Entertainments/catering facilities: Several licensed refreshment points around the ground.

Club shop: Two shops at the ground open on match days.

Handbooks/programmes: Programmes not available on subscription.

Club Colours: Blue shirts, white shorts.

Change Colours: Red shirts, white shorts, red stockings.

Club Nickname: 'Lions'.

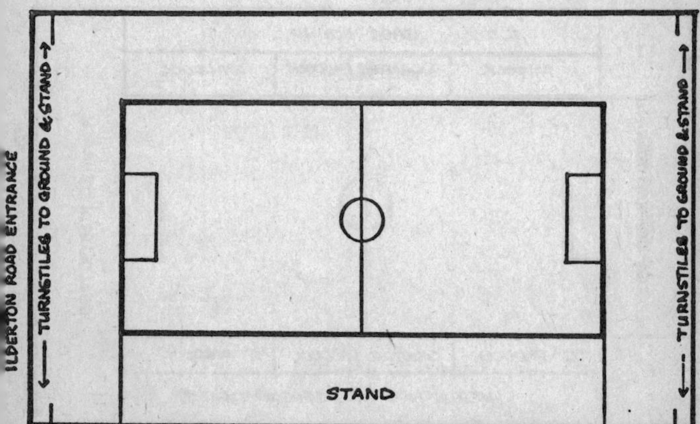

NEWCASTLE UNITED

ST JAMES' PARK, NEWCASTLE-UPON-TYNE NE1 4ST.

TELEPHONE NEWCASTLE 28361/2. ANSWERPHONE 611571.

Telegraphic Address: 'Football, Newcastle-on-Tyne'.

Ground capacity: 56,000 (35,000 covered). **Pitch measurements:** 115 yds × 75 yds. **Address of Supporters' Club:** 2 St. James' Street, Newcastle-upon-Tyne, NE1 4NF.

How to get there: The ground is central and within walking distance of the railway station and the town centre.

Match tickets: Postal and personal applications accepted 10 days before the match.

Car parking: Car park on the north side of the ground. Street parking available.

Entertainments/catering facilities: Excellent facilities in the New Stand. Refreshments available in all parts of the ground.

Club shop: Open weekdays 9.30–5.00 and Saturdays 9.30–3.00. Run by the Development Association.

Handbooks/programmes: Programmes if available can be ordered from the secretary up to three weeks after the match. Handbook published by Supporters' Club.

Club Colours: Black and white striped shirts, black shorts, black and white stockings.

Change Colours: All blue.

Club Nickname: 'Magpies'.

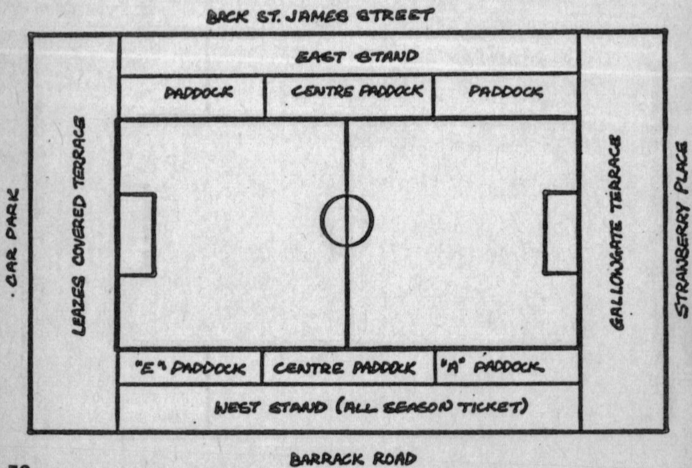

NEWPORT COUNTY

SOMERTON PARK, NEWPORT, MON.

TELEPHONE 71543 AND 71271.

Ground capacity: 22,060 (seating 672). **Pitch measurements:** 112 yds × 78 yds.
Address of Supporters Club: Same as Football Club.

How to get there: Nearest railway station, Newport High St. By bus: the Chepstow Road bus to Beechwood and walk down over Somerton Hill; the Corporation Road bus to Cromwell Road and Somerton Park. All buses from bus centre in Dock Street.

Match tickets: Seats can be reserved from the club secretary.

Car parking: Car park at the back of the Social Club Stand in Cromwell Road. Otherwise street parking.

Entertainments/catering facilities: Licensed bar at Somerton Road end. Licensed bar in the Social Club at Cromwell Road; both membership only. Buffet in the enclosure and on the terrace. Tea bar on the terrace also.

Club shop: Sells all types of souvenirs.

Handbooks/programmes: Back issues of programmes available from programme shop. Club history available from Vice-President's club, Somerton Park.

Club Colours: Tangerine shirts, black shorts, tangerine stockings.

Change Colours: White shirts, black shorts, white stockings.

Club Nickname: 'The Ironsides'.

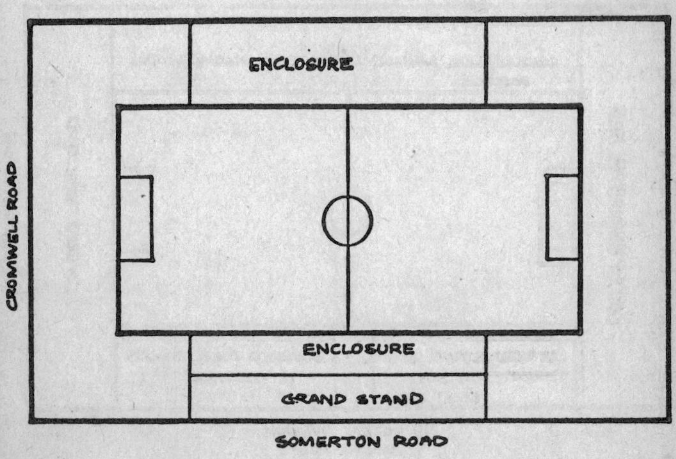

NORTHAMPTON TOWN

COUNTY GROUND, ABINGTON AVENUE, NORTHAMPTON NN1 4PS.
TELEPHONE NORTHAMPTON 37553.

Ground capacity: 21,000 (Seating 1,959). **Pitch measurements:** 120 yds × 75 yds. **Address of Supporters Club:** 195, Abington Avenue, Northampton.

How to get there: Nearest railway station, Castle Station. Any bus to the town centre, then from Mercer's Row, buses 1, 21, 2 and 14, though only 2 goes right to the ground.

Match tickets: Seats can be booked by telephone up to 2 days before the match· personal application, or by post 2 weeks prior to match.

Car parking: No car park, but ample space in nearby side-streets.

Entertainments/catering facilities: Refreshment in hotel and tea bars on ground.

Club shop: Run by the Supporters Club; sells all types of souvenirs.

Handbooks/programmes: Programmes available from the Supporters Club.

Club Colours: White shirts, claret bands round chest, claret shorts and claret and white stockings.

Change Colours: All blue.

Club Nickname: 'Cobblers'.

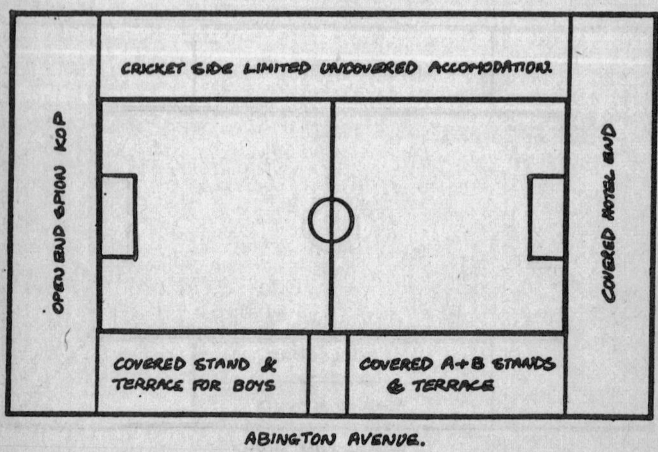

NORWICH CITY

CARROW RD., NORWICH NOR 22.

TELEPHONE NORWICH 21514/5.

Telegraphic address: 'Football, Norwich'.

Ground capacity: 48,000. **Pitch measurements:** 114 yds × 74 yds.

How to get there: Norwich Thorpe railway station is eight minutes walk from the ground; British Rail run trains from outlying districts on match days. Coach firms also operate special services from surrounding parts. Any scheduled bus to the station and then walk.

Match tickets: Personal applications only at the previous first-team match to the Advance Ticket Office on the ground.

Car parking: Several private cars parks within walking distance of the ground. Multi-storey parks in Malt House Road and St Andrews Street. Street parking in Rouen Road, Carrow Hill, Kerrison Road, Cousins Road, and side streets off King Street. Coaches may park at Martineau Lane off the City Ring Road to the south of the city.

Entertainments/catering facilities: Supporters' Club in Rosary Road within walking distance of the ground. Numerous licensed bars in the ground.

Club shop: Sells all types of souvenirs.

Handbooks/programmes: Supporters Club produce a handbook. Programmes available on demand but not on subscription.

Club Colours: Yellow shirts, green collars and cuffs green shorts with yellow stripe, yellow stockings.

Change Colours: All white.

Club Nickname: 'Canaries'.

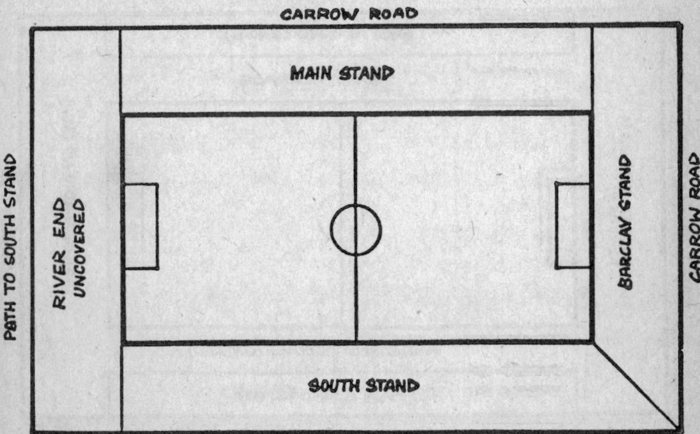

NOTTINGHAM FOREST

CITY GROUND, NOTTINGHAM NG2 5FJ.

TELEPHONE NOTTINGHAM 868236-7-8.

Telegraphic Address: 'Forestball, Nottingham'.

Ground capacity: 49,000 (26,500 covered). **Address of Supporters Club:** 'Forest House', 6 Pavilion Road, West Bridgford, Nottingham.

How to get there: From Nottingham Midland station any bus marked 'Trent Bridge'. Corporation specials from Parliament Street.

Match tickets: Bookable 14 days in advance of the match.

Car parking: Room for 300 cars in the East Stand car park and street parking off the Loughborough and Radcliffe Roads.

Entertainments/catering facilities: Only match-day refreshment bars. Social club situated just outside the ground.

Club shop: Two shops on the ground sell all types of souvenirs.

Handbooks/programmes: Programmes available on subscription from Carrington Publications Ltd., 20 Carrington St., Nottingham.

Club Colours: Red shirts, white shorts, red and white stockings.

Change Colours: All white.

Club Nickname: 'Reds'.

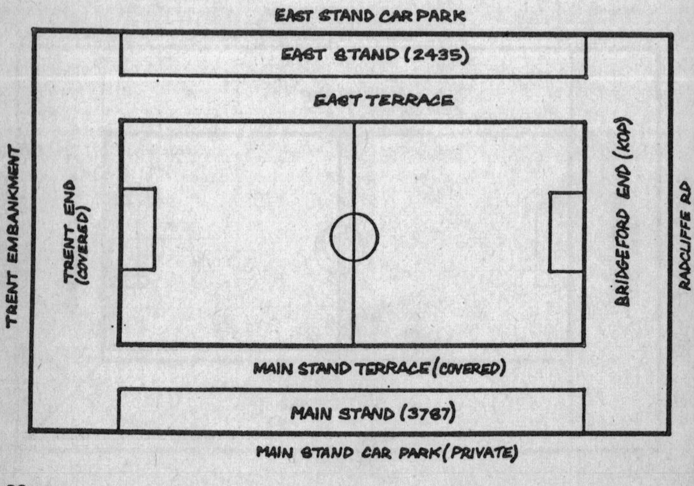

NOTTS COUNTY

COUNTY GROUND, MEADOW LANE, NOTTINGHAM NG2 3HJ.

TELEPHONE SECRETARY: NOTTINGHAM 864152; MANAGER: NOTTINGHAM 868364. TELEX 24549 ANSWER BACK PATRONS.

Telegraphic Address: 'Notts County F.C. Nottingham'.

Ground capacity: 40,000. **Pitch measurements:** 117 yds × 76 yds. **Address of Supporters Club:** c/o Club.

How to get there: Corporation Specials from Parliament Square. Nearest railway station Nottingham Midland; from there any bus marked 'Trent Bridge'.

Match tickets: Advance bookings can be accepted by post or by personal application 14 days before each home game. S.A.E. must be sent with remittance in postal applications.

Car parking: No street parking around the ground, but ample space in the City of Nottingham Corporation car park on the Cattle Market, Meadow Lane, just 400 yards from the main entrances. There is a small club car park at the rear of the Spion Kop on Iremonger Road.

Entertainments/catering facilities: No social club. Tea bars and refreshment points on all sides of the ground.

Club shop: Open only on match days; situated under the Meadow Lane stand.

Handbooks/programmes: No handbooks. Back copies of programmes from the Secretary, Supporters Club, Meadow Lane.

Club Colours: Black and white striped shirts, black shorts, blue and white stockings.

Change Colours: Yellow shirts and green shorts.

Club Nickname: 'Magpies'.

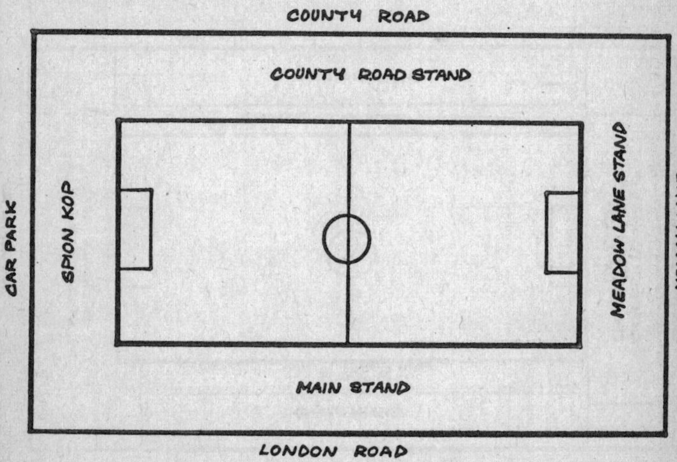

OLDHAM ATHLETIC

BOUNDARY PARK, OLDHAM.

TELEPHONE 061-624-4972.

Ground capacity: 30,000 (16,000 covered). **Pitch measurements:** 110 yds × 74 yds. **Address of Supporters Club:** Same as Football Club.

How to get there: Oldham Werneth is the nearest railway station; ordinary bus routes, and specials link the station to the ground at Boundary Park.

Match tickets: Tickets can be booked in advance and collected on or before the day of the match; or, if required, they can be sent through the post.

Car parking: Parking for 1,000 cars at the Chadderton End of the ground.

Entertainments/catering facilities: A new social club has been built and it holds 350–400 people. It is open after matches and every evening except Mondays, when it is available for private parties. Catering stands around the ground sell hot drinks and pies.

Club shop: A new shop has been opened and sells all the usual souvenirs.

Handbooks/programmes: Programmes on sale at the ground or through the post for 10p plus postage and packing.

Club Colours: Blue shirts, blue shorts, white stockings.

Change Colours: Orange shirts, blue shorts, white stockings.

Club Nickname: 'The Latics'.

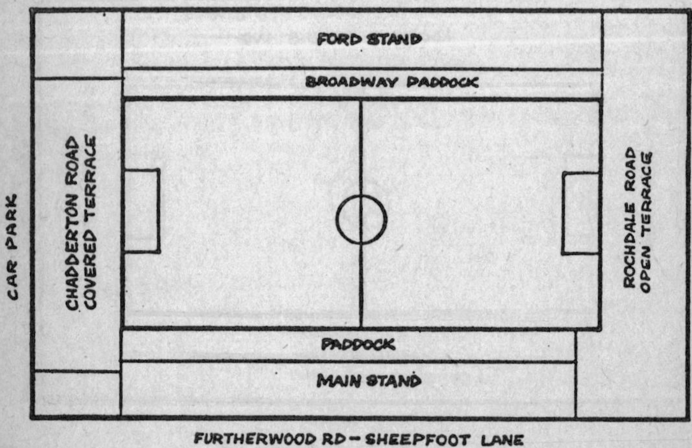

ORIENT

LEYTON STADIUM, BRISBANE ROAD, LEYTON, LONDON, E10 5NE.
TELEPHONE 01-539-2223/4.

Telegraphic Address: 'Orient', Brisbane Road, Leyton London, E.10.

Ground capacity: 33,500 (5000 seats). **Pitch measurements:** 110 yds × 80 yds.
Address of Sportsman's Supporters Club: Same as Ground.

How to get there: Buses 69, 58, 278, 241 pass the ground. From the centre of London, journey by underground (Central Line) to Leyton station; the ground is a few minutes walk. Nearest BR station is Leyton Midland Road (off Oliver Rd.).

Match tickets: Can be booked two weeks in advance.

Car parking: Street parking around the ground. A National Car Park five minutes from Brisbane Road (off Oliver Rd.).

Entertainments/catering facilities: Supporters' Section Club and snack bar points around the ground.

Club shop: Sells all types of souvenirs.

Handbooks/programmes: Programmes can be obtained on subscription, and back numbers can be ordered from the club shop.

Club Colours: Red shirts with white insert, white shorts, black stockings with red and white tops.

Club Nickname: 'The O's'.

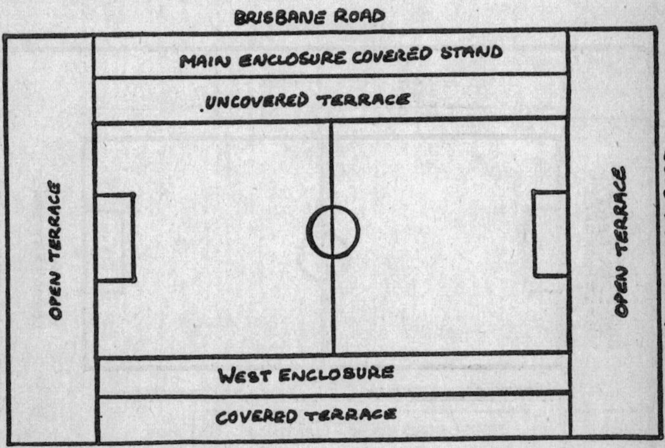

OXFORD UNITED

MANOR GROUND, BEECH ROAD, HEADINGON, OXFORD.

TELEPHONE OXFORD 61503.

Ground capacity: 18,000. **Pitch measurements:** 112 yds × 78 yds. **Address of the Supporters Club:** Supporters Club Offices, Manor Ground, Beech Road, Headington, Oxford.

How to get there: Bus 2 from the city centre. Nearest railway station is Oxford General. From the station take Bus 1 to Queens Lane and then take Bus 2. By road, take Oxford ring road to the east of the city, following the signs for Headington. Leave the ring road at Green Road roundabout into London Road; the ground is on the right after going straight across at the traffic lights.

Match tickets: Subject to availability tickets may be booked 14 days prior to the match.

Car parking: Parking is available in certain streets around the ground.

Entertainments/catering facilities: Cinema, public houses, and cafés, all just minutes from the ground. Refreshments available inside the ground.

Club shop: Open Mon.–Fri. offering all types of souvenirs.

Handbooks/programmes: Handbook and programmes available from the club shop.

Club Colours: All gold.

Change Colours: All white.

Club Nickname: 'The Dons'.

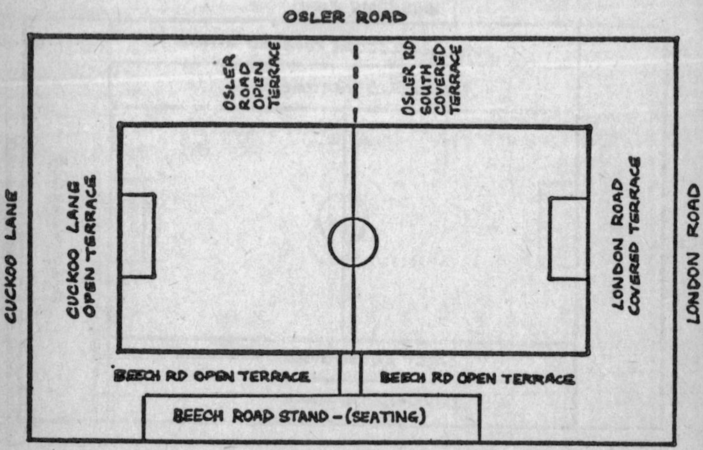

PETERBOROUGH UNITED

LONDON ROAD GROUND, PETERBOROUGH PE2 8AL.
TELEPHONE PETERBOROUGH (0733) 63947.

Ground capacity: 30,000. **Pitch measurements:** 112 yds × 76 yds. **Address of Supporters Club:** Same as Football Club.

How to get there: Peterborough North Station (20 minutes' walking distance). Bus terminus 400 yards.

Match tickets: Bookable 14 days in advance.

Car parking: Ample parking available at the ground.

Entertainments/catering facilities: Supporters' Club provides entertainments. Licensed refreshment kiosks in the ground.

Club shop: Sells all types of souvenirs (postal requests to Commercial Manager).

Handbooks/programmes: Handbooks available and programmes can be ordered on subscription.

Club Colours: Royal blue shirts and shorts, red stockings.

Change Colours: Yellow shirts, royal blue shorts, yellow stockings.

Club Nickname: 'The Posh'.

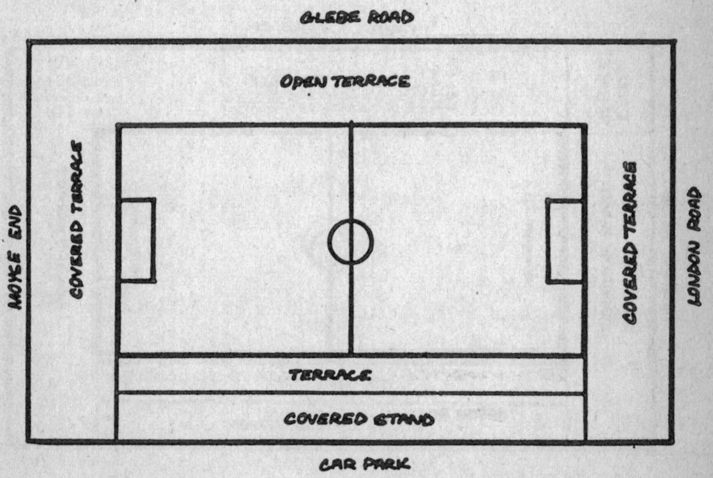

PLYMOUTH ARGYLE

HOME PARK, PLYMOUTH, DEVON.
TELEPHONE PLYMOUTH (0752) 52561/2/3.

Ground capacity: 40,000 (30,000 covered). **Pitch measurements:** 112 yds × 75 yds. **Address of Supporters Association:** Same as Football Club.

How to get there: Special City buses from the Plymouth bus station at Bretonside. Nearest railway station, Plymouth.

Match tickets: Grand Stand and Mayflower Stand tickets are available 2–3 weeks before each first-team game.

Car parking: Car park adjoining the ground holds 2,000 cars.

Entertainments:/catering facilities: Eight refreshment bars around the ground.

Club shop: Situated on the ground; sells all types of souvenirs.

Handbooks/programmes: Handbook published annually and sold by the Supporters Association. Programmes sent to all parts of the world.

Club Colours: Green and white striped shirts, black shorts, white stockings.

Club Nickname: 'The Pilgrims'.

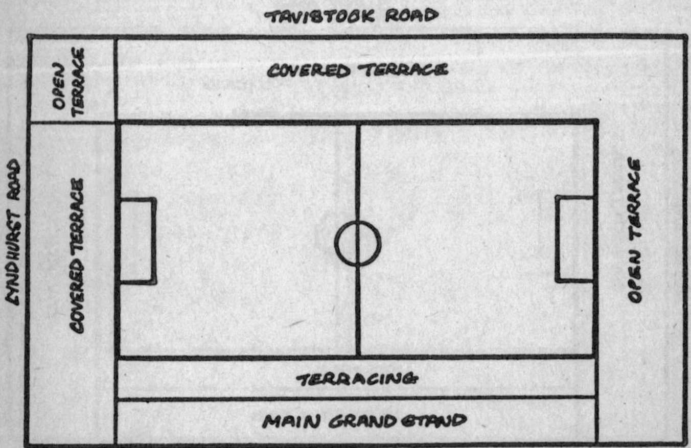

PORTSMOUTH

FRATTON PARK, FROGMORE RD., PORTSMOUTH PO4 8RA.
TELEPHONE PORTSMOUTH 31204/5.

Telegraphic Address: 'Pompey Portsm'th'.

Ground capacity: 46,000 (14,200 covered). **Pitch measurements:** 116 yds × 73 yds.

How to get there: Fratton station on main line from London Waterloo is just four minutes walk from the ground. Buses 17 and 18 from Portsmouth Harbour station and Gosport Ferry Terminal to the ground. Buses also from Portsmouth station.

Match tickets: South Stand centre section (the best seats) bookable 10 days in advance.

Car parking: Only side-street parking.

Entertainments/catering facilities: Pre-match schoolboy football at start and end of season. The Pompey public house and reception rooms adjoin the ground and are owned by the club. The Supporters' Club is open to members of the visiting Supporters' Club before and after the match. There are also several bars around the ground.

Club shop: Two shops in the ground sell all types of souvenirs.

Handbooks/programmes: No handbook. The match-day magazine available on subscription.

Club Colours: White shirts with two blue vertical stripes, blue shorts, white socks with red and blue trim.

Change Colours: Red shirts with two white vertical stripes, white shorts, red socks with blue and white trim.

Club Nickname: 'Pompey'.

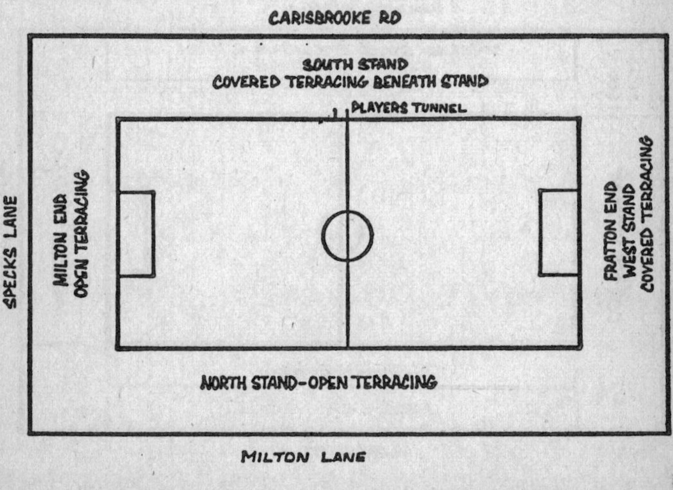

PORT VALE

VALE PARK, BURSLEM, STOKE-ON-TRENT.

TELEPHONE STOKE ON TRENT 87626 AND 85524.

Telegraphic Address: 'Port Vale Burslem'.

Ground capacity: 50,000. **Pitch measurements:** 116 yds × 76 yds. **Address of Supporters Club:** Hamil Rd., Burslem, Stoke on Trent, ST6 1AW.

How to get there: Nearest railway station, Stoke; there are frequent bus services from the town centre to Burslem.

Match tickets: Not bookable in advance.

Car parking: Parking is available behind the Railway Stand on Hamil Road, and on the Lorne Street side of the ground.

Entertainments/catering facilities: Light refreshments served on the ground. Social club on the Hamil Road side of the ground provides entertainment on certain evenings; membership by subscription.

Club shop: Sells all types of souvenirs.

Handbooks/programmes: Programmes are available on application to the club office or to the club shop.

Club Colours: White shirts, black shorts.

Change Colours: Old gold shirts, black shorts.

Club Nickname: 'Valiants'.

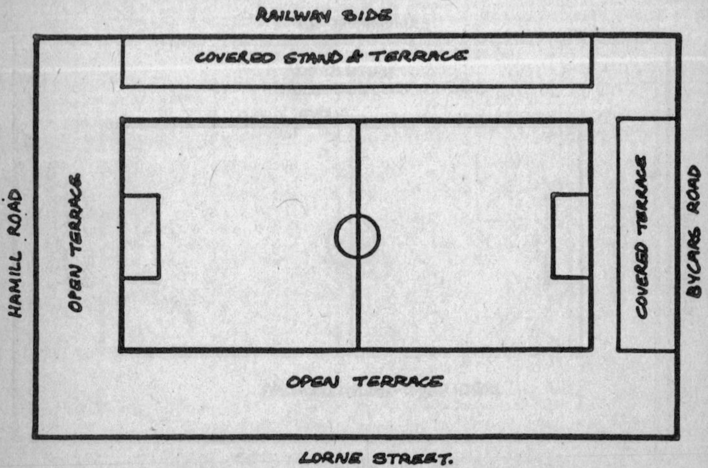

PRESTON NORTH END

DEEPDALE, PRESTON PR1 6RU.

TELEPHONE PRESTON 53818 AND 53819.

Telegraphic Address: 'Football Preston'.

Ground capacity: 40,100. **Pitch measurements:** 112 yds × 78 yds. **Address of Supporters Club:** Deepdale Road, Preston.

How to get there: Special buses to Deepdale from outlying areas and town centre bus station. Nearest railway station: Preston.

Match tickets: Postal applications, including remittance and S.A.E. may be made 14 days before the match.

Car parking: Club car park on the Deepdale Road (West Stand) side of the ground, holds 1,000 vehicles. Only limited off-street parking.

Entertainments/catering facilities: Entertainments provided by the Supporters Club. The ground is well-equiped for normal match-day refreshments.

Club shop: Open on match days. All postal enquiries to: The Commercial Manager, Preston North End Development Association, Deepdale Road, Preston (Tel: Preston 56500).

Handbooks/programmes: No handbook. Programmes available on subscription from the Commercial Manager.

Club Colours: White shirts, with blue collars and cuffs, white shorts with blue stripes, blue stockings, with white rings.

Change Colours: Red and black striped shirts and white shorts.

Club Nickname: 'The Lilywhites'.

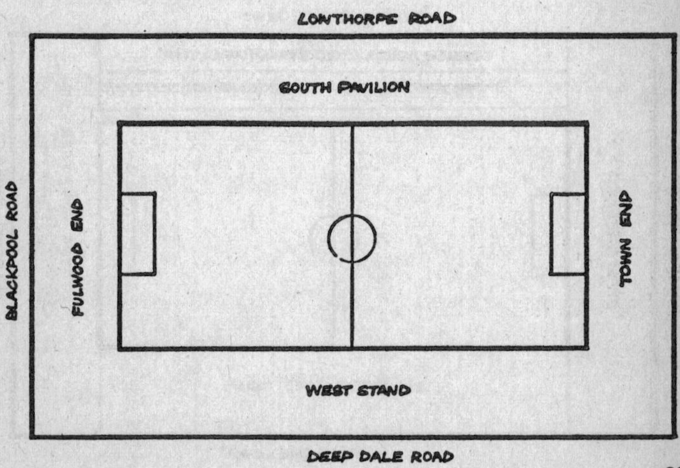

QUEEN'S PARK RANGERS

SOUTH AFRICA ROAD, W12 7PA.

TELEPHONE 01-743-2618.

Telegraphic Address: 'Queu Pear'.

Ground capacity: 30,000 (23,000 covered). **Pitch measurements:** 112 yds × 72 yds, **Address of Supporters Club:** c/o Football Club.

How to get there: Buses 12 and 207. Nos. 11, 49, 72, 88, 105, 220 go near Shepherd's Bush (Metropolitan and Central Lines) and White City (Central Line—five to ten minutes walk).

Match tickets: Seats bookable one month in advance of the match.

Car parking: No club car park, but the White City park, adjacent to the ground, is recommended. Limited parking in side-streets.

Entertainments/catering facilities: Various bars around the ground.

Club shop: Programmes shop in South Africa Road and kiosks inside the ground.

Handbooks/programmes: Available from programme shop.

Club Colours: Blue and white hooped shirts, white shorts, white stockings.

Change Colours: Red and white quartered shirts, black shorts, red socks.

Club Nickname: 'Rangers' or 'R's or 'Superhoops'.

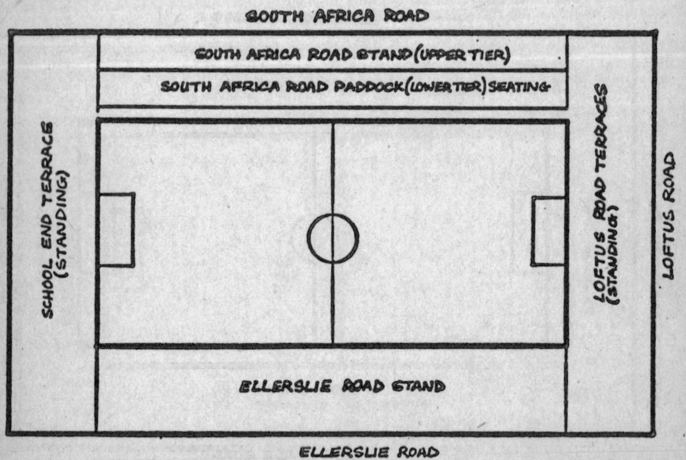

READING

ELM PARK, NORFOLK ROAD, READING.

TELEPHONE READING 57878/9/0.

Ground capacity: 27,000. **Pitch measurements:** 112 yds × 77 yds. **Address of Supporters Club:** Reading Football Supporters Club, Elm Park, Norfolk Road, Reading.

How to get there: Corporation specials from St. Mary's Butts (town centre) and from Northumberland Avenue. Usual buses within a few minutes of the ground. Nearest railway station, Reading General.

Match tickets: Stand tickets are bookable in advance for all first-team matches 14 days before the match.

Car parking: Space is available for approximately 300 cars adjoining the ground entrance in Norfolk Road and Tilehurst Road.

Entertainments/catering facilities: Catering is available in each of the five stands and also on the terraces.

Club shop: Shops in Norfolk Road and on the West Terrace are open on match days selling all types of souvenirs.

Handbooks/programmes: The Supporters Club produce a handbook and these are available on application to the club. Unsold programmes are available after each match at the programme shop on the West Terrace.

Club Colours: Blue and white hoops, white shorts, white stockings, two blue rings.

Change Colours: Yellow and blue.

Club Nickname: 'Biscuitmen'.

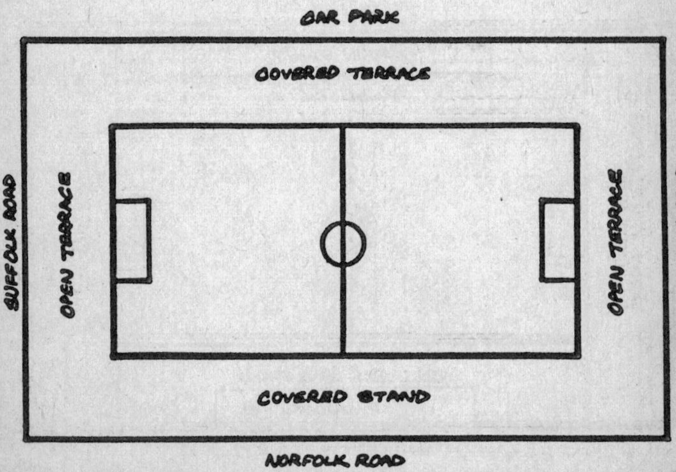

ROCHDALE

SPOTLAND, WILLBUTTS LANE, ROCHDALE.

TELEPHONE 44648/9.

Ground capacity: 28,000. **Pitch measurements:** 113 yds × 75 yds.

How to get there: Football specials run from The Esplanade in the town centre, which is five minutes' walk from Rochdale railway station. Specials also run from the same place for evening matches.

Match tickets: Seats can be reserved in advance.

Car parking: Car parking at the ground and in the adjacent side-streets.

Entertainments/catering facilities: A social club in the car park.

Club shop: Sells all types of souvenirs.

Handbooks/programmes: Programmes not available on subscription.

Club Colours: Royal blue shirts with white trimmings, white shorts with blue stripe, blue stockings.

Change Colours: Yellow shirts, blue shorts, yellow stockings.

Club Nickname: 'The Dale'.

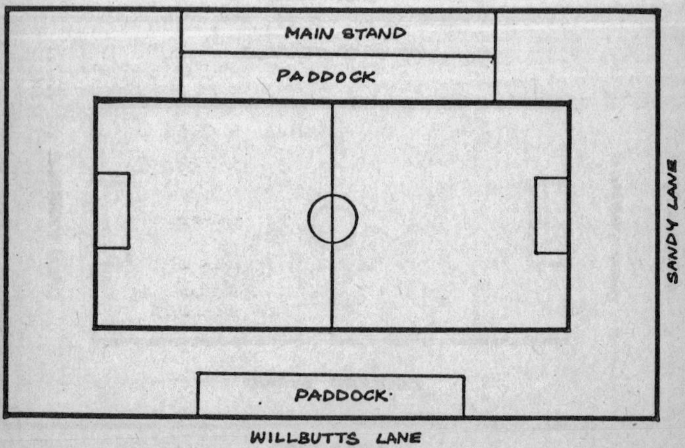

ROTHERHAM UNITED

MILLMOOR GROUND, ROTHERHAM.

TELEPHONE ROTHERHAM 2434.

Telegraphic Address: 'Holmes Millmoor, Rotherham'.

Ground capacity: 24,000. **Pitch measurements:** 115 yds × 76 yds. **Address of Supporters Club:** Red and White Shop, c/o Millmoor, Rotherham.

How to get there: Corporation buses from town centre. Also regular service buses from Sheffield to town centre. Nearest railway stations, Rotherham Masboro and Rotherham Central on the line from Sheffield Midland.

Match tickets: Seats can be reserved one month before the match.

Car parking: There are parks in Kimerworth Road and Main St. (the municipal car park); both are within easy reach of the ground.

Entertainments/catering facilities: There are refreshment kiosks on all four sides of the ground and also behind the grandstand.

Club shop: Sited on the forecourt of the ground; stocks all types of souvenirs.

Handbooks/programmes: No handbook, but programmes may be obtained from the club or the club shop.

Club Colours: Red shirts, white collar, white sleeves, white shorts, red stockings.

Change Colours: All white, blue or yellow.

Club Nickname: 'The Merry Millers'.

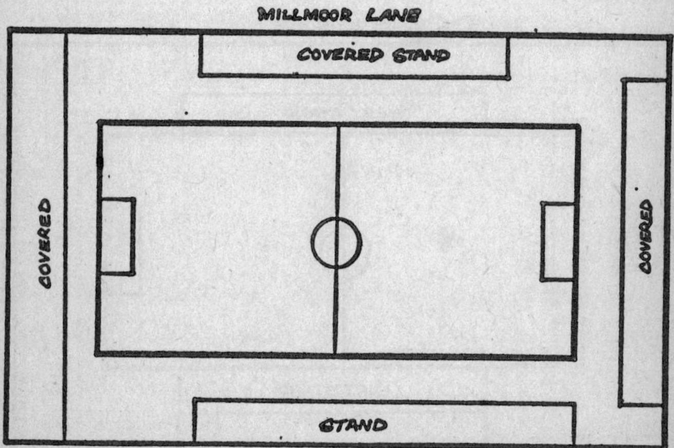

SCUNTHORPE UNITED

OLD SHOW GROUND, SCUNTHORPE, LINCS.

TELEPHONE SCUNTHORPE 2954.

Ground capacity: 27,000. **Pitch measurements:** 112 yds × 78 yds. **Address of Supporters Club:** Scunthorpe U. Supporters and Social Club at Ground.

How to get there: Buses 211, 212, 213, 118 run near the ground. Nearest railway station is Scunthorpe. By road along A18 from Doncaster via Berkley Circle. Doncaster Road Hill, and Henderson Avenue; A18 from Grimsby; A15 from Lincoln via Queensway Circle, Ashby Road, Station Roundabout, Church Lane, Exeter Road, and Doncaster Road; via A1 on A638 to Retford to A620 to Gainsborough, A159 to Scunthorpe.

Match tickets: Tickets are bookable up to the day before the match unless advertised otherwise in the local press. No telephone bookings accepted.

Car parking: Club car park adjoining the ground holds 40–50 cars. Ample street parking around the ground.

Entertainments/catering facilities: Catering sub-let to an outside firm; hot drinks and light refreshments served on first-team match days.

Club shop: Three club shops on the ground sell all types of souvenirs.

Handbooks/programmes: Programmes available on match days.

Club Colours: All red.

Change Colours: All blue.

Club Nickname: 'The Irons'.

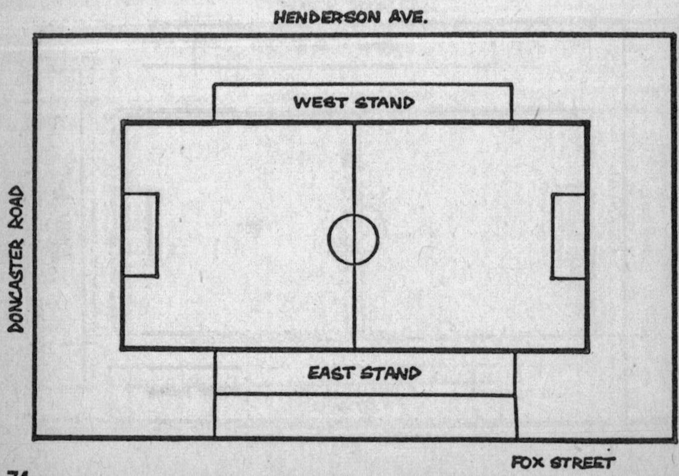

SHEFFIELD UNITED

BRAMALL LANE GROUND, SHEFFIELD, S2 4SU.

TELEPHONE SHEFFIELD 25585.

Telegraphic Address: 'United, Sheffield'.

Ground capacity: 55,000. **Pitch measurements:** 115 yds × 73 yds. **Address of Supporters Club:** Secretary, 247 Ormond Road, Sheffield S8 8FT.

How to get there: Buses 34, 35, 38, 42, 45 from the central bus station. Sheffield Midland railway station is within walking distance of the town centre.

Match tickets: Tickets bookable 14 days prior to the match.

Car parking: The ground is five minutes from car parks in the city centre. Ample parking in side-streets around Bramall Lane.

Entertainments/catering facilities: Pre-match lunch can be obtained in the Lane Social Club restaurant. Numerous bars and buffets in the ground.

Club shop: Sells all types of souvenirs.

Handbooks/programmes: Mail order service available through the club shop.

Extra information: Lane Social Club offers restaurant, lounge bars, bier keller, sauna baths, and keep-fit facilities.

Club Colours: Red and white striped shirts, black shorts, white stockings, two red bands on top.

Change Colours: All white, white stockings with two red bands at top.

Club Nickname: 'Blades'.

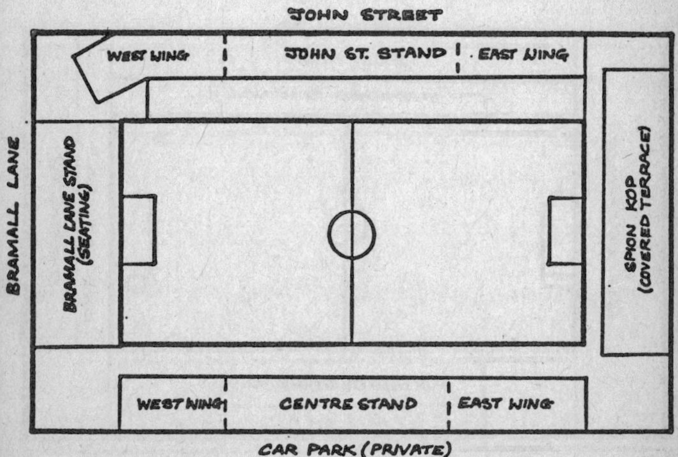

SHEFFIELD WEDNESDAY

HILLSBOROUGH SHEFFIELD, S6 1SW.

TELEPHONE SHEFFIELD 343123. (BOX OFFICE: SHEFFIELD 343122).

Telegraphic Address: 'Wednesday, Sheffield 6 .

Ground capacity: 60,000. **Pitch measurements:** 115 yds × 75 yds. **Address of Supporters Club:** Same as ground.

How to get there: Buses 42, 53, 81, 2 from the city centre. Sheffield Midland railway station is close to the centre.

Match tickets: Seats can be booked in advance in the South and North Stands. Postal applications to the Box Office not more than 21 days before the match. Tickets are offered subject to being unsold when the application is received. Remittance and S.A.E. must be enclosed.

Car parking: Street parking available. Also a park at the training ground in Middlewood Road.

Entertainments/catering facilities: Refreshment bars in all parts of the ground.

Club shop: Two shops in the ground sell all types of souvenirs.

Handbooks/programmes: Handbooks available from the secretary. Programmes available on subscription.

Club Colours: Royal blue/white striped shirts, royal blue shorts, white stockings.

Change Colours: Yellow shirts and socks, blue shorts.

Club Nickname: 'Owls'.

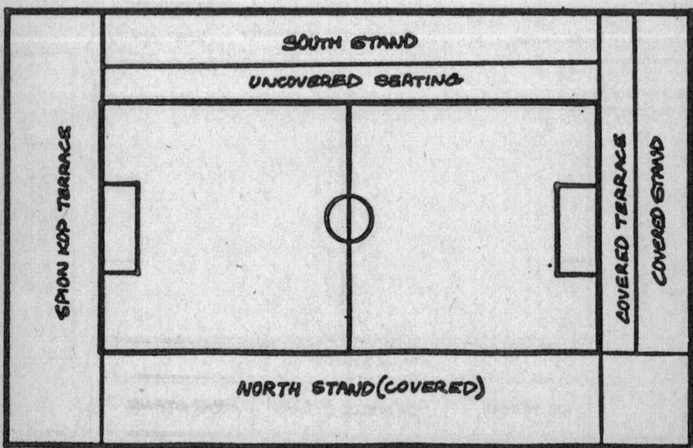

SHREWSBURY TOWN

GAY MEADOW, SHREWSBURY.

TELEPHONE SHREWSBURY 56068.

Ground capacity: 20,050. **Pitch measurements:** 116 yds × 76 yds. **Address of Supporters Club:** c/o Football Club.

Hot to get there: Midland Red schedule bus services from main bus station in Barker Street to the ground. Special coach facilities are arranged by local companies from neighbouring districts. Shrewsbury railway station is 10 minutes walk from the ground.

Match tickets: Tickets can be booked by post two weeks prior to the match by sending correct remittance and S.A.E. Reservation can also be made by post two days before the match.

Car parking: A park adjacent to the ground and a free public car park five minutes walk away.

Entertainments/catering facilities: Buffets are situated on each side of the ground.

Club shop: Sells all types of souvenirs.

Handbooks/programmes: No handbook. Programmes can be obtained through the post at 10p each plus S.A.E.

Club Colours: Blue with amber trim.

Change Colours: Amber with blue trim.

Club Nickname: 'Town'.

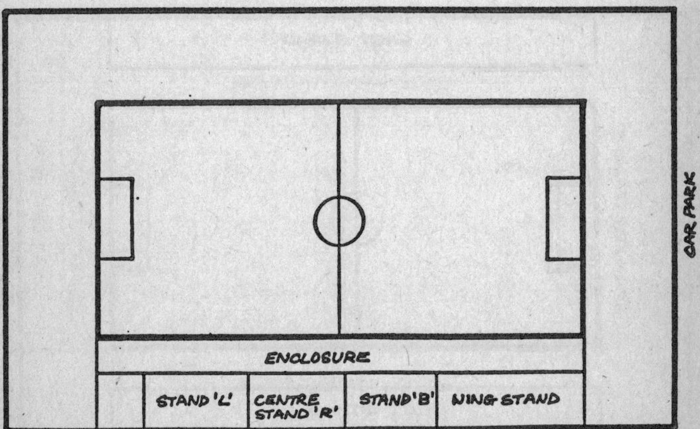

SOUTHAMPTON

THE DELL, MILTON ROAD, SOUTHAMPTON SO9 4XX.

TELEPHONE SOUTHAMPTON 23408.

Ground capacity: 31,000. **Pitch measurements:** 110 yds × 72 yds. **Address of Supporters Club:** Same as Football Club.

How to get there: The ground is 10 minutes walk from Southampton Central station via Hill Lane. Buses 2 and 5 from the city centre pass the ground, which is only 10 minutes walk from the centre.

Match tickets: No seats available, all seats being sold to season-ticket holders. Room on the terraces for 24,000 standing, and admission is through the turnstiles on the day of the match.

Car parking: Only street parking in the vicinity of the ground. Municipal car parks in the city centre.

Entertainments/catering facilities: Licensed bars inside the ground.

Club shop: Situated in the private car park alongside the ground.

Handbooks/programmes: Handbooks not published annually. Programmes available on subscription.

Club Colours: Red and white striped shirts, black shorts, red and white stockings.

Change Colours: Gold shirts, blue shorts, gold stockings.

Club Nickname: 'Saints'.

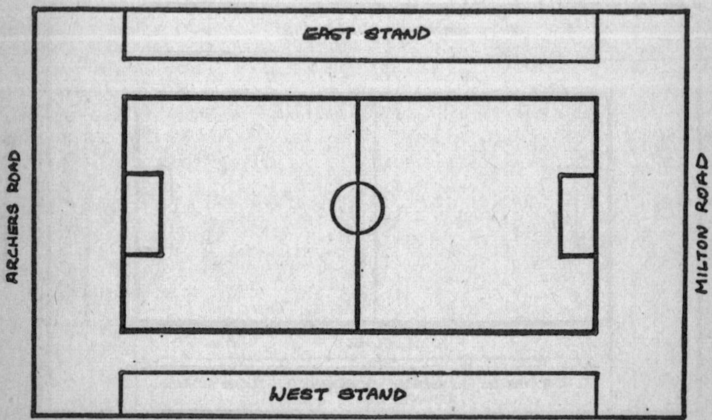

SOUTHEND UNITED

ROOTS HALL FOOTBALL GROUND, VICTORIA AVENUE, SOUTHEND-ON-SEA.

TELEPHONE SOUTHEND 40707.

Ground capacity: 35,000 (16,000 covered). **Pitch measurements:** 110 yds × 74 yds. **Address of Supporters Club:** 374 Victoria Ave., Southend-on-Sea, Essex.

How to get there: Regular buses from Southend Central station in the High Street; the station is on the London line from Fenchurch Street. Southend Victoria, five minutes walk from the ground, is served by trains from Liverpool Street, London.

Match tickets: Seats can be purchased 14 days before the match.

Car parking: Two car parks at the ground hold approximately 700 cars. Ample parking in side-streets.

Entertainments/catering facilities: Tea bars all around the ground. There is a social club for members and *bona fide* visitors.

Club shop: Situated in Victoria Avenue opposite the ground; sells all types of souvenirs.

Handbooks/programmes: Both handbooks and programmes are available from the club shop; programmes are available on subscription.

Club Colours: Royal blue shirts, blue shorts, with white stripes, white stockings.

Change Colours: All white.

Club Nickname: 'The Shrimpers'.

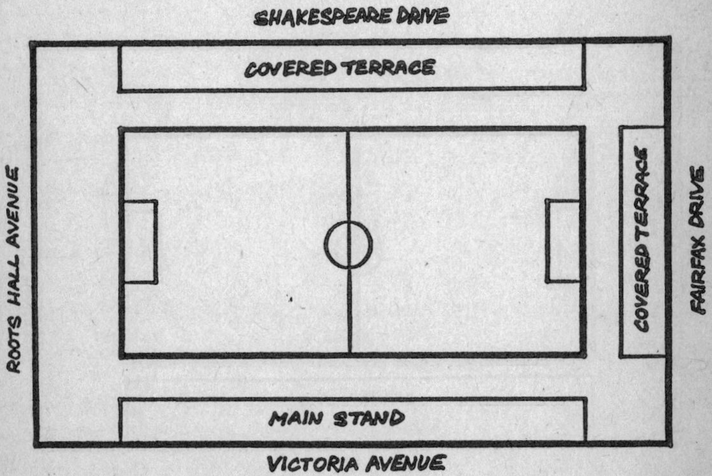

SOUTHPORT

HAIG AVENUE, SOUTHPORT PR8 6JZ.

TELEPHONE SECRETARY, SOUTHPORT 33422; MANAGER, SOUTHPORT 36321.

Ground capacity: 21,000 (11,000 covered). **Pitch measurements:** 113 yds × 77 yds. **Address of Supporters Club:** c/o The Ground.

How to get there: Special buses from south town centre (near Southport main railway station). By road; from Liverpool via Formby by-pass, town centre, Palace cinema, Eastbank, Scarisbrick New Road, to Haig Avenue; from Liverpool via Maghull and Halsall as above; from Preston and the North via town centre and Scarisbrick New Road.

Match tickets: Reserved seats for special matched only.

Car parking: Certain side-streets are available.

Entertainments/catering facilities: Kiosks on the ground.

Club shop: Sells all types of souvenirs.

Handbooks/programmes: No handbook. Programmes available on subscription.

Club Colours: Old gold shirts, royal blue shorts and gold stockings.

Change Colour: All red.

Club Nickname: 'The Sandgrounders'.

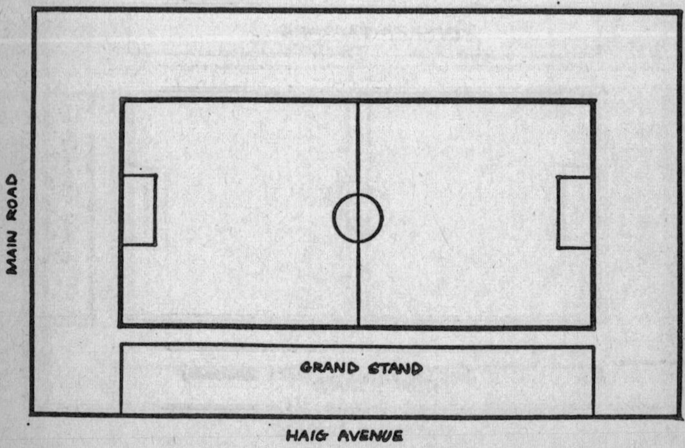

STOCKPORT COUNTY

EDGELEY PARK, STOCKPORT, CHESHIRE, SK3 9DD.

TELEPHONE STOCKPORT 8888/9.

Ground capacity: 24,904. **Pitch measurements:** 110 yds × 75 yds. **Address of Supporters Club:** Same as Football Club.

How to get there: Edgeley Park is situated within a mile of Mersey Square, the town centre; a few minutes walk via Wellington Road South and Greek Street. The main line railway station lies just off Greek Street and is only five minutes from the ground. By road, there are RAC signs to ground on all the main routes around the town centre.
Match tickets: Seats can be reserved in the Main Stand by post or telephone two weeks before the match.
Car parking: Ample street parking around the ground.
Entertainments/catering facilities: Modern licensed club adjoining the ground.
Club shop: Adjacent to the ground; sells all types of souvenirs.
Handbooks/programmes: Programmes available for match only.
Club Colours: White shirts, blue collars, white shorts, white stockings with blue ring at top.
Change Colours: Blue and black striped shirts, black shorts, black and blue stockings.
Club Nickname: 'The Hatters'.

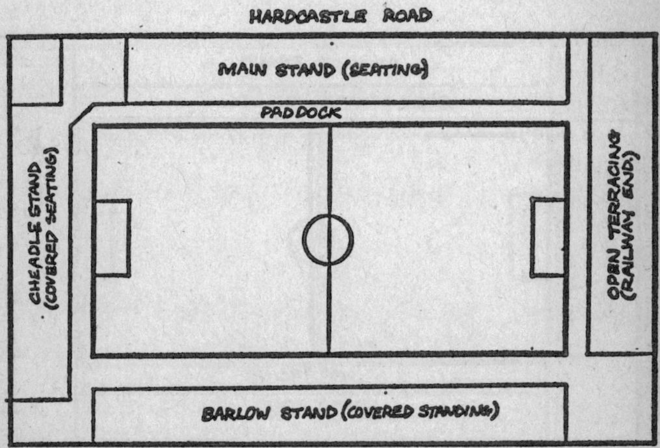

STOKE CITY

VICTORIA GROUND, STOKE-ON-TRENT.

TELEPHONE STOKE-ON-TRENT 44660.

Telegraphic Address: 'Football, Stoke-on-Trent'.

Ground capacity: 50,500. **Pitch measurements:** 116 yds × 75 yds.

How to get there: Stoke-on-Trent railway station, on the main line from London, is five minutes walk from the ground. No special buses from the town centre because the ground is central. By road, Stoke is well served by the M6 which passes just two miles from the city.

Match tickets: Bookable two weeks before the match.

Car parking: The official car park in Wheildon Road holds 2,000 cars. Street parking permitted.

Entertainments/catering facilities: Social club. Refreshments obtainable on the ground.

Club shop: Sells all types of souvenirs.

Handbooks/programmes: Programmes available on subscription.

Club Colours: Red and white striped shirts, white shorts and stockings.

Change Colours: White shirts, black shorts, white stockings

Club Nickname: 'Potters'.

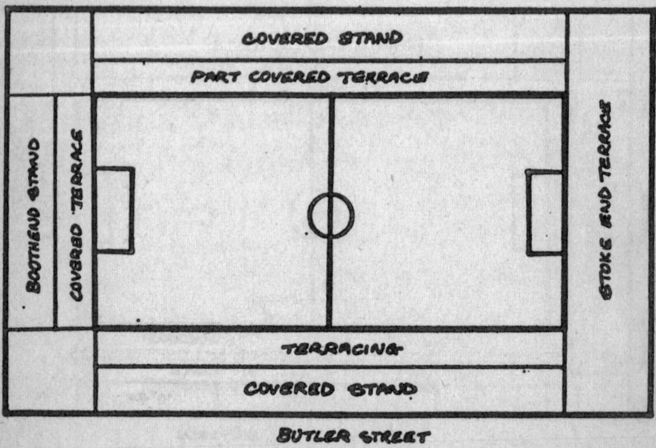

SUNDERLAND

ROKER PARK GROUND, SUNDERLAND.

TELEPHONE SUNDERLAND 72077 AND 58638.

Telegraphic Address: 'Football, Sunderland'.

Ground capacity: 53,500. **Pitch measurements:** 112 yds × 72 yds. **Address of the Supporters Club:** c/o Roker Park.

How to get there: From Sunderland railway station and Seaburn railway station take buses 23 and 24 to Redby Community Centre: the ground is five minutes walk away. Special buses from the town centre. By road via M1, A690 to Sunderland, and then route to Roker Park is signed.

Match tickets: Seats may be booked 10 days prior to the match.

Car parking: Limited parking close to the ground.

Entertainments/catering facilities: Hot and cold drinks, pies, sandwiches, etc. available in the ground.

Club shop: Open on match days; sells all types of souvenirs.

Handbooks/programmes: Programmes and the club newspaper, the *Roker Times*, are obtainable on subscription; details from the club offices.

Club Colours: Red and white striped shirts, black shorts, red stockings with white tops.

Change Colours: All white, with single red and black stripe on shirt.

Club Nickname: 'Rokerites'.

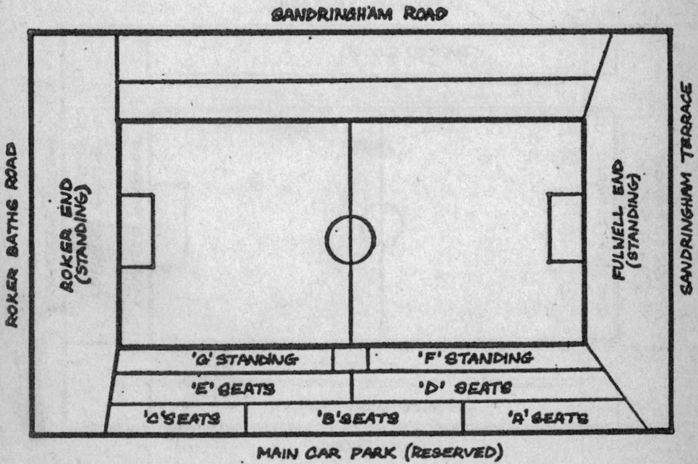

SWANSEA CITY

VETCH FIELD, SWANSEA.

TELEPHONE SWANSEA 53633.

Ground capacity: 35,000. **Pitch measurements:** 110 yds × 70 yds. **Address of Supporters Club:** Elysium Buildings, High Street, Swansea.

How to get there: 10 minutes' walk from bus depot. South Wales Transport Co. Ltd. services from High Street General station to Lower Oxford Street.

Match tickets: Tickets can be reserved in advance.

Car parking: Car park 200 yards from the ground in The Kingsway. Side-street parking available.

Entertainments/catering facilities: Disc jockey programme prior to the match. Licensed bar and refreshment kiosk inside the ground.

Club shop: Situated in William Street; sells all types of souvenirs.

Handbooks/programmes: No handbook. Programmes can be obtained from the Secretary by sending remittance and S.A.E.

Club Colours: All white.

Change Colours: All red, with white collars.

Club Nickname: 'Swans'.

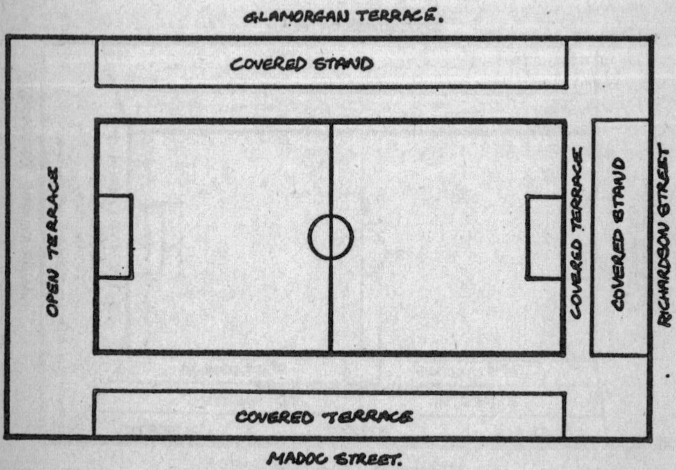

SWINDON TOWN

COUNTY GROUND, SWINDON, WILTSHIRE.

TELEPHONE GROUND SWINDON 22118; TRAINING GROUND SWINDON 6623.

Ground capacity: 28,000 (6500 seats). **Pitch measurements:** 117 yds × 78 yds.
Address of Supporters Club: Swindon Town Supporters Club, County Ground, Swindon, Wilts.

How to get there: Both Swindon bus and railway stations are half a mile from the ground.

Match tickets: Available 3 weeks in advance.

Car parking: Corporation car park adjacent to the west end of the ground, off County Road.

Club shop: Postal enquiries welcome. All types of souvenirs are stocked.

Handbooks/programmes: Programmes available by postal application, but not on subscription.

Entertainments/catering facilities: The Members' Club. Rendezvous Club in the North Stand. Refreshment kiosks in all parts of the ground.

Club Colours: Red shirts, white shorts, red and white stockings.

Change Colours: All blue with blue and white stockings.

Club Nickname: 'Robins'.

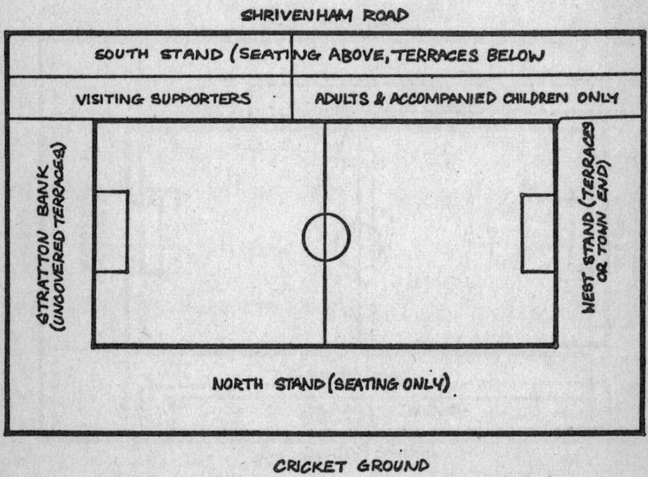

TORQUAY UNITED

PLAINMOOR GROUND, TORQUAY, DEVON. TQ1 3PS.

TELEPHONE TORQUAY 38666–7 (STD CODE 0803).

Ground capacity: 22,000. **Pitch measurements:** 112 yds × 74 yds. **Address of Supporters Association:** Plainmoor, Torquay, Devon.

How to get there: Train to Torquay railway station. Bus 30 runs every 12 minutes from the station to the ground.

Match tickets: Stand seats available a fortnight before the match. Postal applications accepted provided correct remittance and S.A.E. are enclosed.

Car parking: Some street parking. Coaches park at Lymington Road coach station.

Entertainments/catering facilities: The Gull Club—a match-day venue luxury club—membership £1 (48 hours notice required for membership). Supporters' social club open all week—membership 50p (48 hours notice required for membership).

Club shop: Sells all types of souvenirs.

Handbooks/programmes: For programmes contact the club shop.

Club Colours: All white with blue/yellow stripes on shorts.

Change Colours: Yellow shirts, blue shorts, yellow stockings.

Club Nickname: 'The Gulls'.

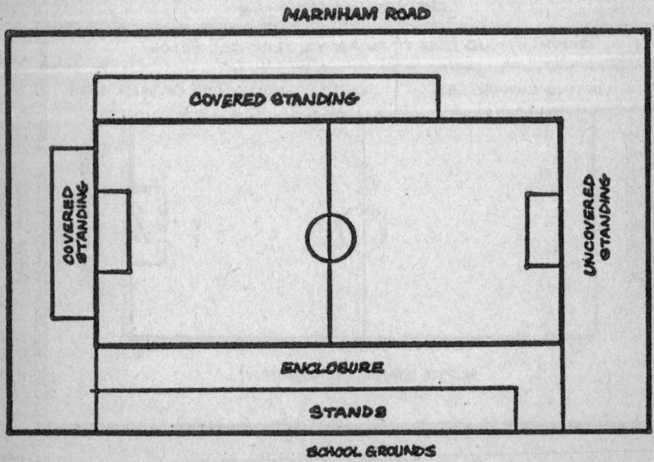

TOTTENHAM HOTSPUR

748 HIGH RD., TOTTEHNAM, N.17.

TELEPHONE 01-808-2046.

Ground capacity: 56,000. **Pitch measurements:** 110 yds × 73 yds. **Address of Supporters Club:** 744 High Road, London N.17.

How to get there: Underground to Manor House (Piccadilly line) or Seven Sisters (Victoria line). From Manor House, buses 279, 259; from Seven Sisters 67 149, 171, 243, 259, 123, 279. White Hart Lane station is three minutes walk from the ground and is served by trains from Liverpool St.

Match tickets: For League matches, seats can be booked not earlier than 21 days before the match. At the Park Lane and Paxton Road ends, there are seats available at the turnstiles.

Car parking: No street parking within a ¼ mile radius of the ground.

Entertainments/catering facilities: Hot food available at snack and chicken bars in the ground.

Club shop: There is a shop 100 yards from the ground, and a kiosk at the East End which stocks over 400 items.

Handbooks/programmes: Programmes available on subscription to shop.

Club Colours: White shirts, blue shorts, white stockings.

Change Colours: Yellow shirts, white shorts and stockings.

Club Nickname: 'Spurs'.

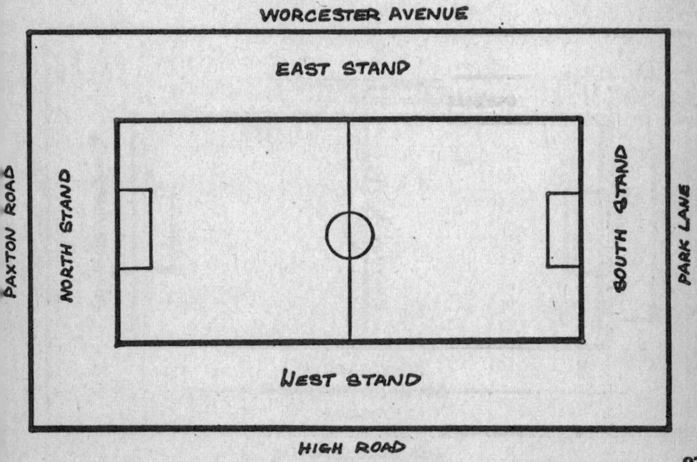

TRANMERE ROVERS

PRENTON PARK, 14 PRENTON ROAD WEST, BIRKENHEAD.

TELEPHONE 051-608-3677/4194.

Ground capacity: 25,000. **Pitch measurements:** 112 yds × 74 yds. **Address of Supporters Club:** Supporters Assn., Prenton Park, West Birkenhead.

How to get there: Special buses from railway stations, Hamilton Square and Rock Ferry. Mersey Railway, Liverpool, to Hamilton Square, then buses 80 to 90 or 64.

Match tickets: Seats can be booked in advance.

Car parking: Large car park at the back of the stand.

Entertainments/catering facilities: Snack bars in ground. Social club with bar facilities.

Club shop: Run by Supporters' Association.

Handbooks/programmes: Programmes available on subscription.

Club Colours: All white with blue facings, blue shorts and white stockings with blue tops.

Change Colours: All red.

Club Nickname: 'Rovers'.

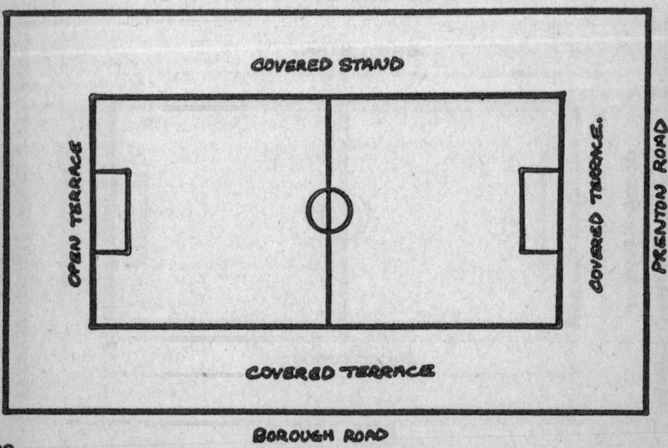

WALSALL

FELLOWS PARK, WALSALL.

TELEPHONE 0922 22791.

Telegraphic Address: 'Walsall F.C., Walsall',

Ground capacity: 24,100. **Pitch measurements:** 113 yds × 73 yds. **Address of Supporters Club:** 61 Bradford Street, Walsall, Staffs.

How to get there: Corporation specials from Bradford Place. Buses 37 and 38 within walking distance of the ground. Nearest railway stations, Bescot (10 minutes' walk from ground) and Walsall.

Match tickets: Seats can be booked at any time by postal, personal, or telephone application to the secretary's office.

Car parking: Car park in Hillary Street for 200 cars. Side-street parking available.

Entertainments/catering facilities: Supporters club adjacent to stadium. Four tea bars and three licensed bars inside the ground.

Club shop: The Boutique, run by the Supporters' Club, is open on match days.

Handbooks/programmes: Yearly handbook published. Programmes available on subscription.

Club Colours: White shirts with red facings, red shorts, white stockings.

Change Colour: Blue shirts, black shorts, blue stockings.

Club Nickname: 'Saddlers'.

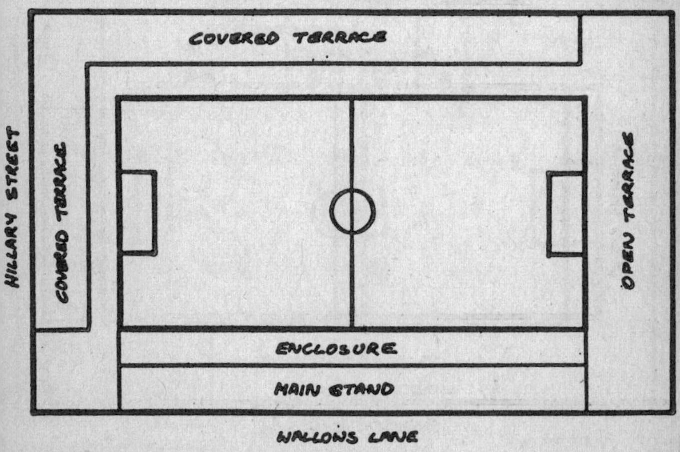

WATFORD

VICARAGE ROAD GROUND, WATFORD. WD1 8ER.

TELEPHONE WATFORD 21759.

Ground capacity: 36,500. **Pitch measurements:** 113 yds × 73 yds. **Address of Supporters Club:** Watford F.C. Supporters Club, Vicarage Road, Watford.

How to get there: Bus 385 from Watford Junction. This and Watford High Street station are both within walking distance of the ground. Trains from London leave Euston station.

Match tickets: Stand seats bookable 10 days before each League match. The Police insist that visiting supporters who wish to stand must use the Vicarage Road end.

Car parking: Parking for season-tickets holders only at the ground, but there are several multi-storey car parks a few minutes away (charge 10p).

Entertainments/catering facilities: Tea kiosks and hot dog stands inside the ground.

Club shops: Four shops on the ground sell all types of souvenirs.

Handbooks/programmes: Handbook produced annually, price 5p, and programmes are available on subscription.

Club Colours: Gold shirts, black shorts, gold stockings.

Change Colours: All red.

Club Nickname: 'Hornets'.

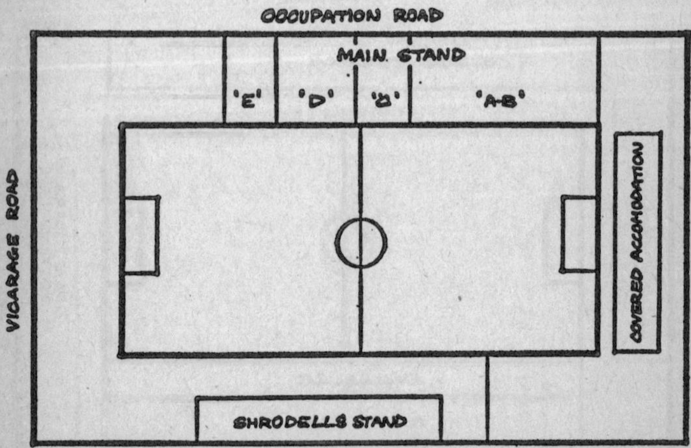

WEST BROMWICH ALBION

THE HAWTHORNS, WEST BROMWICH.

TELEPHONE 021-553 0095. BOX OFFICE 021-553-5472.

Ground capacity: 50,500. **Pitch measurements:** 115 yds × 75 yds. **Address of Supporters Club:** Throstle Club, Birmingham Road, West Bromwich, Staffs.

How to get there: Buses 72, 74, 75, and 79 from outside Birmingham New Street station run directly to the ground. A special bus service from the centre of West Bromwich to the ground runs every three minutes on match days.

Match tickets: Advance bookings for Centre and Wing Stands accepted six weeks in advance by post including remittance and S.A.E. Telephone bookings are accepted but not before two days prior to the match; tickets reserved by telephone must be collected at least 30 minutes before kick-off. A limited number of unreserved seats in the Paddock are available at Door E1 on the day of the match.

Car parking: Street parking permitted in certain areas, all within 10 minutes walk of the ground.

Entertainments/catering facilities: Post-match entertainment in the Supporters' Club adjoining the ground. Excellent facilities at the Hawthorns Throstle Club alongside the ground includes a full course lunch; several restaurants within walking distance of the ground. Snack bars in the ground.

Club shop: Situated in the Pools Office in Halfords Lane, and open from 9–5 Mon.–Sat. Stocks over 150 different articles.

Handbooks/programmes: No handbook. Programmes available on subscription.

Club Colours: Navy blue and white striped shirts, white shorts and white stockings.

Change Colours: Yellow and green striped shirts, blue shorts, yellow stockings.

Club Nickname: 'Baggies', 'Throstles' 'Albion'.

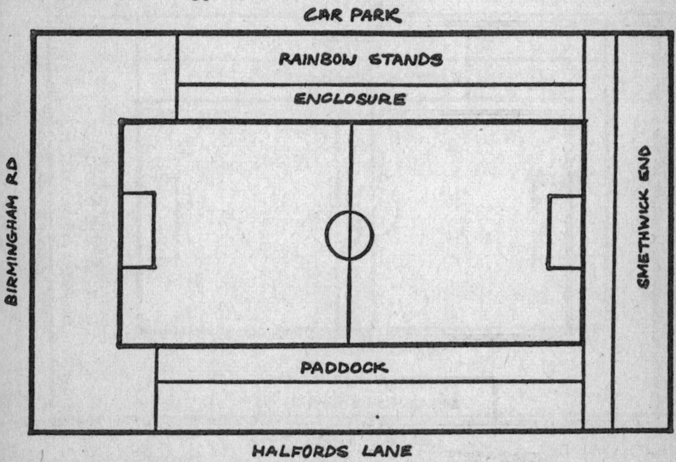

WEST HAM UNITED

BOLEYN GROUND, GREEN STREET, UPTON PARK, LONDON E.13.
TELEPHONE 01-472-7004.

Ground capacity: 41,000. **Pitch measurements:** 110 yds × 70 yds. **Address of Supporters Club:** Castle St., Upton Park, E.13.

How to get there: Nearest station Upton Park (Underground, District Line)—five minutes' walk. Buses from Barking Road, Romford Road and Green Street.

Match tickets: Advance booking, by personal application only, 12 days prior to League matches.

Car parking: Ample side-street parking available.
Entertainments/catering facilities: Refreshment points around the ground.

Club shop: Situated on the ground; sells all types of souvenirs.

Handbooks/programmes: Handbook published. Programmes available by post from either Sales Service c/o West Ham United F.C. or from Helliar & Sons, 237, Barking Road, London E13 8EQ.

Club Colours: Claret shirts, blue sleeves, white shorts and white stockings.

Change Colours: Sky blue shirts with two claret bands, sky blue shorts and stockings.

Club Nickname: 'Hammers'.

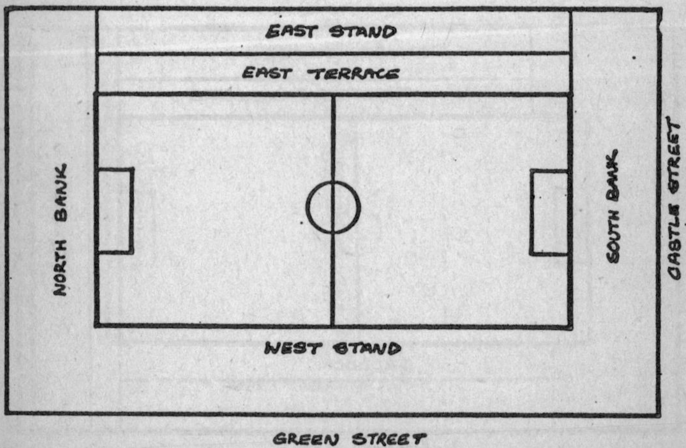

WOLVERHAMPTON WANDERERS

MOLINEUX GROUNDS, WOLVERHAMPTON.

TELEPHONE WOLVERHAMPTON 24053/4.

Telegraphic Address: 'Wanderers, Wolverhampton .

Ground capacity: 53,500. **Pitch measurements:** 115 yds × 72 yds.

How to get there: The ground is within easy walking distance of both Wolverhampton High Level railway station and the town centre. For this reason the local bus company does not operate special services on match days.

Match tickets: Seats are bookable by post one month before the match.

Car parking: Parking is available around 'The West Park', in various side streets, and at the Molineux Hotel (10p per match).

Entertainments/catering facilities: Entertainment at the Wolves Social Club a few yards from the ground. Bars are provided all around the ground.

Club shop: The club shop is situated on the official car park at the ground.

Handbooks/programmes: No handbook. Programmes available on subscription.

Club Colours: Old gold shirts, black collar and cuffs, black shorts, old gold stockings.

Change Colours: White shirt, black shorts, white stockings.

Club Nickname: 'Wolves'.

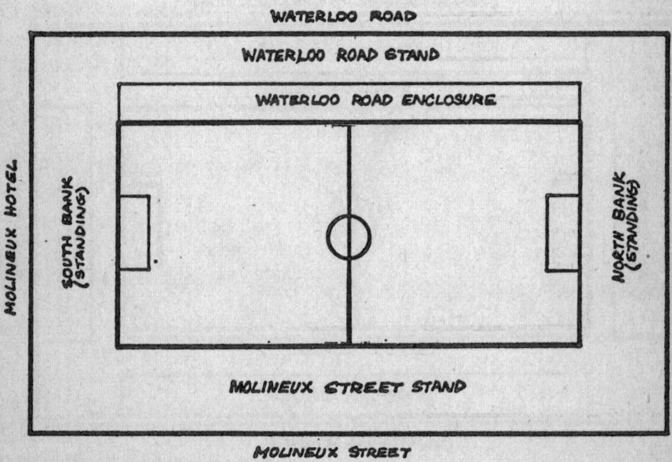

WORKINGTON

BOROUGH PARK, WORKINGTON.
TELEPHONE WORKINGTON 2871.

Telegraphic Address: 'Borough Park, Workington'.

Ground capacity: 21,000 (10,000 covered). **Pitch measurements:** 112 yds × 76 yds. **Address of Supporters Club:** R. Dawes (Secretary), 10 The Crescent, Keswick, Cumbria.

How to get there: Buses from Maryport and Carlisle to the ground. Nearest railway station, Workington.

Match tickets: Tickets can be booked in advance from the club secretary.

Car parking: Park adjacent to the ground holds 1,000 cars.

Entertainments/catering facilities: Social club under the main stand. Canteen on popular side of the ground.

Club shop: Sells all types of souvenirs.

Handbooks/programmes: Programmes not sold on subscription, but the club will supply back numbers. when possible.

Club Colours: Red shirts, white shorts.

Change Colours: All sky blue.

Club Nickname: 'The Reds'.

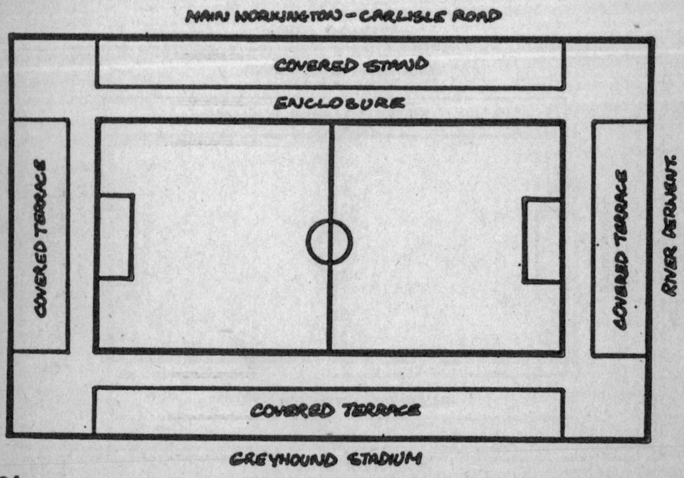

WREXHAM

RACECOURSE GROUND, MOLD ROAD, WREXHAM.

TELEPHONE WREXHAM 2414.

Telegraphic Address: 'Football, Wrexham'.

Ground capacity: 36,000 (18,000 covered). **Pitch measurements:** 117 yds × 75 yds. **Address of Supporters Club:** Secretary, John Roberts, 10, Sandringham Rd.

How to get there: Wrexham General railway station is only 200 yards from the ground. Trains run from Chester and Shrewsbury. Bus services from outlying districts to town.

Match tickets: Stand tickets bookable in advance.

Car parking: Parking grounds at St Marks, Bodyhfryd Square, Eagles Meadows, Old Guild Hall, Hill Street, Holt Street, and Town Hill, Hill Street.

Entertainments/catering facilities: A social club and four catering kiosks at the ground.

Club shop: Situated on the Kop side of the ground; stocks all types of souvenirs.

Handbooks/programmes: No handbook at present. Programmes available on subscription.

Club Colours: Red shirts with white facings, white shorts with red stripe.

Change Colours: Sky blue shirts, white shorts and stockings.

Club Nickname: 'The Robins'.

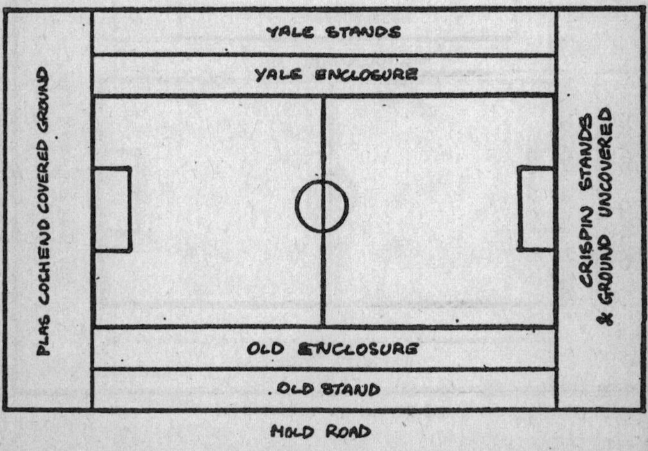

YORK CITY

BOOTHAM CRESCENT, YORK.

TELEPHONE: YORK 24447.

Telegraphic Address: 'City Football Club, York'.

Ground capacity: 17,000. **Pitch measurements:** 115 yds × 75 yds. **Address of Supporters Club:** Same as Football Club.

How to get there: Buses 2 and 8 every 10 minutes from York railway station to the ground.

Match tickets: On sale 14 days prior to game. Sales cease 48 hours prior to game, and then re-open immediately prior to game.

Car parking: Ample parking in side-streets.

Entertainments/catering facilities: Licensed social club (members only). Three tea bars on the ground.

Club shop: Selling all types of souvenirs.

Handbooks/programmes: Programmes not available on subscription.

Club Colours: Maroon shirts with white 'Y' on front, white shorts, maroon stockings.

Change Colours: Same as above, colours reversed.

Club Nickname: 'Minster Men'.

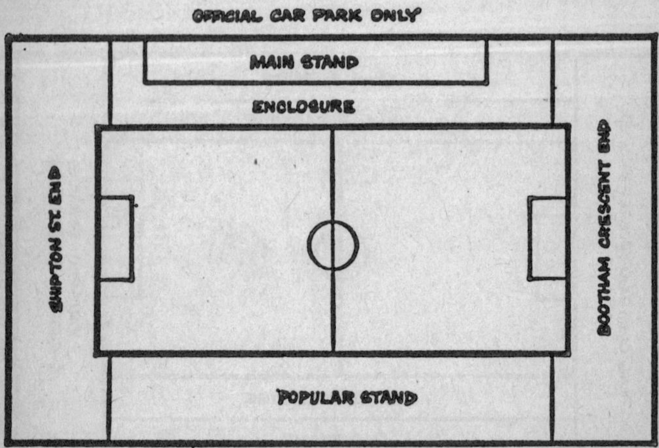

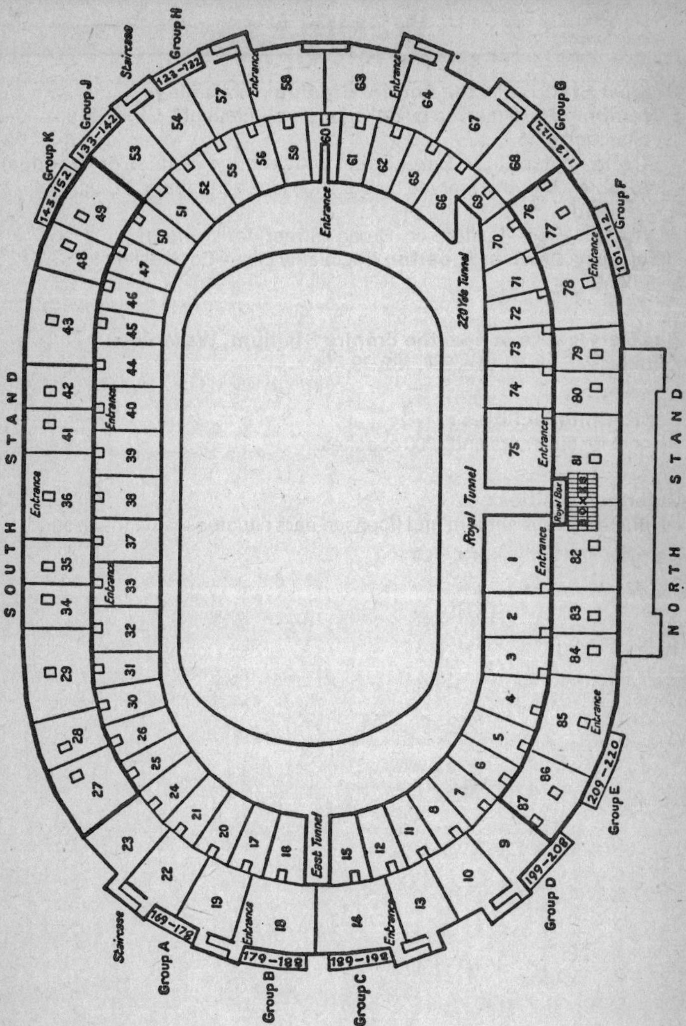
SOUTH STAND
NORTH STAND
Royal Tunnel
220 Yds Tunnel
East Tunnel
Royal Box
Entrance
Staircase
Group A
169–178
Group B
179–188
Group C
189–198
Group D
199–208
Group E
209–220
Group F
101–112
Group G
113–122
Group H
123–132
Group J
133–142
Group K
143–152

WEMBLEY

Nearest Stations to the Empire Stadium, Wembley:

Wembley Park (served by Bakerloo Line—Elephant & Castle to Stanmore)
(Metropolitan Line—Baker Street to Aylesbury, Watford, or Uxbridge)

Wembley Central (served by Bakerloo Line—Elephant & Castle to Watford)
(British Rail—Euston or Broad Street to Watford).

Sudbury Town or Alperton (Piccadilly Line—Cockfosters to Uxbridge).

Bus Services to or near the Empire Stadium, Wembley:

Routes 245, 18, 83, 92a, 297, 182, 79, 79a.

Car Parking facilities:

Room for 6000 cars and 1000 coaches.

Catering facilities:

Numerous refreshment and licensed bars situated inside the ground.

Football League Fixtures 1975/76

(*Subject to alteration*)

Saturday, August 16 1975

DIVISION ONE
Aston Villa v Leeds U.
Burnley v Arsenal
Everton v Coventry C.
IpswichT v Newcastle U.
Leicester C. v Birmingham C.
Manchester C. v Norwich C.
Q.P.R. v Liverpool
Sheffield U. v Derby Co.
Stoke C. v West Ham U.
Tottenham H. v Middlesbrough
Wolverhampton W. v Manchester U.

DIVISION TWO
Bristol C. v Bolton W.
Carlisle U. v Oxford U.
Charlton Ath. v Notts Co.
Fulham v Blackpool
Luton T. v Hull C.
Nottingham F. v Plymouth Arg.
Oldham Ath. v Bristol R.
Orient v Blackburn R.
Southampton v W.B.A.
Sunderland v Chelsea
York C. v Portsmouth

DIVISION THREE
Brighton & H.A. v Rotherham U.
Bury v Gillingham
Crystal Palace v Chester
Grimsby T. v Cardiff C.
Halifax T. v Millwall
Hereford U. v Port Vale
Mansfield T. v Shrewsbury T
Peterborough U. v Walsall
Preston N.E. v Colchester U.
Southend U. v Sheffield W.
Swindon T. v Chesterfield
Wrexham v Aldershot

DIVISION FOUR
Barnsley v Watford
Bradford C. v Brentford
Darlington v Scunthorpe U.
Doncaster R. v Cambridge U.
Exeter C. v Southport
Hartlepool v AFC Bournemouth
Huddersfield T. v Northampton T.
Newport Co. v Lincoln C.
Reading v Rochdale
Stockport Co. v Crewe Alex.
Swansea C. v Tranmere R.
Torquay U. v Workington

Tuesday, August 19 1975

DIVISION ONE
Birmingham C. v Manchester U.
Burnley v Everton
Coventry C. v Derby Co.
Liverpool v West Ham U.
Q.P.R. v Aston Villa
Sheffield U. v Arsenal
Stoke C. v Wolverhampton W.
Tottenham H. v Ipswich T.

DIVISION TWO
Bristol C. v Sunderland
Fulham v Carlisle U.
Hull C. v Blackpool
Orient v Notts Co.

Wednesday, August 20 1975

DIVISION ONE
Manchester C. v Leicester C.
Newcastle U. v Middlesbrough
Norwich C. v Leeds U.

DIVISION TWO
Oxford U. v Bolton W.
W.B.A. v Chelsea

Saturday, August 23 1975

DIVISION ONE
Arsenal v Stoke C.
Birmingham C. v Everton
Coventry C. v Manchester C.
Derby Co. v Q.P.R.
Leeds U. v Ipswich T.
Liverpool v Tottenham H.
Manchester U. v Sheffield U.
Middlesbrough v Wolverhampton W.
Newcastle U. v Leicester C.
Norwich C. v Aston Villa
West Ham U. v Burnley

DIVISION TWO
Blackburn R v Oldham Ath.
Blackpool v Orient
Bolton W. v Fulham
Bristol R. v York C.
Chelsea v Carlisle U.
Hull C. v Bristol C.
Notts Co. v Southampton
Oxford U. v Sunderland
Plymouth Arg. v Charlton Ath.
Portsmouth v Nottingham F.
W.B.A. v Luton T.

DIVISION THREE
Aldershot v Halifax T.
Cardiff C. v Bury
Chester v Southend U.
Chesterfield v Crystal Palace
Colchester U. v Mansfield T.
Gillingham v Grimsby T.
Millwall v Wrexham
Port Vale v Preston N.E.
Rotherham U. v Hereford U.
Sheffield W. v Brighton & H.A.
Shrewsbury T. v Peterborough U.
Walsall v Swindon T.

DIVISION FOUR
AFC Bournemouth v Darlington
Brentford v Hartlepool
Cambridge U. v Bradford C.
Crewe Alex. v Reading
Lincoln C. v Torquay U.
Northampton T. v Stockport Co.
Rochdale v Swansea C.
Scunthorpe U. v Exeter C.
Southport v Barnsley
Tranmere R. v Doncaster R.
Watford v Huddersfield T.
Workington v Newport Co.

Monday, August 25 1975
DIVISION ONE
West Ham U. v Tottenham H.

Tuesday, August 26 1975
DIVISION ONE
Arsenal v Norwich C.
Everton v Sheffield U.
Ipswich T. v Burnley
Leeds U. v Liverpool
Middlesbrough v Birmingham C.
Wolverhampton W. v Q.P.R.

DIVISION TWO
Charlton Ath. v Orient
Southampton v Bristol C.
Sunderland v Fulham

Wednesday, August 27 1975
DIVISION ONE
Aston Villa v Manchester C.
Derby Co. v Newcastle U.
Leicester C. v Stoke C.
Manchester U. v Coventry C.

DIVISION TWO
Chelsea v Oxford U.

Friday, August 29 1975
Charlton Ath. v Oxford U.
Orient v Portsmouth
Southampton v Plymouth Arg.

DIVISION FOUR
Exeter C. v Tranmere R.

Saturday, August 30 1975
DIVISION ONE
Aston Villa v Coventry C.
Burnley v Middlesbrough
Everton v Derby Co.
Ipswich T. v Birmingham C.
Leicester C. v Liverpool
Manchester C. v Newcastle U.
Q.P.R. v West Ham U.
Sheffield U. v Leeds U.
Stoke C. v Manchester U.
Tottenham H. v Norwich C.
Wolverhampton W. v Arsenal

DIVISION TWO
Bristol C. v Bristol R.
Carlisle U. v Blackburn R.
Fulham v W.B.A.
Luton T. v Chelsea
Nottingham F. v Notts Co.
Oldham Ath. v Hull C.
Sunderland v Blackpool
York C. v Bolton W.

DIVISION THREE
Brighton & H.A. v Cardiff C.
Bury v Aldershot
Crystal Palace v Colchester U.
Grimsby T. v Shrewsbury T.
Halifax T. v Walsall
Hereford U. v Sheffield W.
Mansfield T. v Chester
Peterborough U. v Port Vale
Preston N.E. v Millwall
Southend U. v Rotherham U.
Swindon T. v Gillingham
Wrexham v Chesterfield

DIVISION FOUR
Barnsley v Northampton T.
Bradford C. v AFC Bournemouth
Darlington v Watford
Doncaster R. v Crewe Alex.
Hartlepool v Lincoln C.
Huddersfield T. v Rochdale
Newport Co. v Scunthorpe U.
Reading v Southport
Stockport Co. v Workington
Swansea C. v Cambridge U.
Torquay U. v Brentford

Saturday, September 6 1975
DIVISION ONE
Arsenal v Leicester C.
Birmingham C. v Q.P.R.
Coventry C. v Ipswich T.
Derby Co. v Burnley
Leeds U. v Wolverhampton W.
Liverpool v Sheffield U.
Manchester U. v Tottenham H.
Middlesbrough v Stoke C.
Newcastle U. v Aston Villa

Norwich C. v Everton
West Ham U. v Manchester C.

DIVISION TWO
Blackburn R. v Bristol C.
Blackpool v Oldham Ath.
Bolton W. v Southampton
Bristol R. v Charlton Ath.
Chelsea v Nottingham F.
Hull C. v Orient
Notts Co. v Carlisle U.
Oxford U. v Fulham
Plymouth Arg. v Sunderland
Portsmouth v Luton T.
W.B.A. v York C.

DIVISION THREE
Aldershot v Mansfield T.
Cardiff C. v Crystal Palace
Chester v Grimsby T.
Chesterfield v Peterborough U
Colchester U. v Halifax T.
Gillingham v Preston N.E.
Millwall v Hereford U.
Port Vale v Brighton & H.A.
Rotherham U. v Bury
Sheffield W. v Wrexham
Shrewsbury T. v Swindon T.
Walsall v Southend U.

DIVISION FOUR
AFC Bournemouth v Doncaster R.
Brentford v Barnsley
Cambridge U. v Stockport Co.
Crewe Alex. v Torquay U.
Lincoln C. v Reading
Northampton T. v Bradford C.
Rochdale v Newport Co.
Scunthorpe U. v Huddersfield T.
Southport v Swansea C.
Tranmere R. v Darlington
Watford v Hartlepool
Workington v Exeter C.

Saturday, September 13 1975
DIVISION ONE
Aston Villa v Arsenal
Burnley v Norwich C.
Everton v Newcastle U.
Ipswich T. v Liverpool
Leicester C. v West Ham U.
Manchester C. v Middlesbrough
Q.P.R. v Manchester U.
Sheffield U. v Coventry C.
Stoke C. v Leeds U.
Tottenham H. v Derby Co.
Wolverhampton W. v Birmingham C.

DIVISION TWO
Bristol C. v Oxford U.
Carlisle U. v Portsmouth
Charlton Ath. v Blackpool
Fulham v Bristol R.
Luton T. v Bolton W.
Nottingham F. v Hull C.
Oldham Ath. v Chelsea
Orient v Plymouth Arg.
Southampton v Blackburn R.
Sunderland v W.B.A.
York C. v Notts Co.

DIVISION THREE
Brighton & H.A. v Chester
Bury v Chesterfield
Crystal Palace v Rotherham U.
Grimsby T. v Millwall
Halifax T. v Shrewsbury T.
Hereford U. v Colchester U.
Mansfield T. v Cardiff C.
Peterborough U. v Aldershot
Preston N.E. v Walsall
Southend U. v Port Vale
Swindon T. v Sheffield W.
Wrexham v Gillingham

DIVISION FOUR
Barnsley v Crewe Alex.
Bradford C. v Tranmere R.
Darlington v Northampton T.
Doncaster R. v Brentford
Exeter C. v Cambridge U.
Hartlepool v Scunthorpe U.
Huddersfield T. v Lincoln C.
Newport Co. v Southport
Reading v Watford
Stockport Co. v AFC Bournemouth
Swansea C. v Workington
Torquay U. v Rochdale

Saturday September 20 1975
DIVISION ONE
Arsenal v Everton
Birmingham C. v Burnley
Coventry C. v Stoke C.
Derby Co. v Manchester C.
Leeds U. v Tottenham H.
Liverpool v Aston Villa
Manchester U. v Ipswich T.
Middlesbrough v Q.P.R.
Newcastle U. v Wolverhampton W.
Norwich C. v Leicester C.
West Ham U. v Sheffield U.

DIVISION TWO
Blackburn R. v Sunderland
Blackpool v Southampton
Bolton W. v Orient
Bristol R. v Carlisle U.
Chelsea v Bristol C.
Hull C. v Fulham
Notts Co. v Luton T.
Oxford U. v Nottingham F.
Plymouth Arg. v York C.
Portsmouth v Oldham Ath.
W.B.A. v Charlton Ath.

DIVISION THREE

Aldershot v Preston N.E.
Cardiff C. v Halifax T.
Chester v Peterborough U.
Chesterfield v Hereford U.
Colchester U. v Brighton & H.A.
Gillingham v Mansfield T.
Millwall v Southend U.
Port Vale v Swindon T.
Rotherham U. v Wrexham
Sheffield W. v Grimsby T.
Shrewsbury T. v Crystal Palace
Walsall v Bury

DIVISION FOUR

AFC Bournemouth v Newport Co.
Brentford v Stockport Co.
Cambridge U. v Huddersfield T.
Crewe Alex. v Darlington
Lincoln C. v Exeter C.
Northampton T. v Swansea C.
Rochdale v Bradford C.
Scunthorpe U. v Torquay U.
Southport v Hartlepool
Tranmere R. v Barnsley
Watford v Doncaster R.
Workington v Reading

Monday, September 22 1975

DIVISION THREE

Port Vale v Cardiff C.
Southend U. v Preston N.E.

DIVISION FOUR

Stockport Co. v Darlington
Tranmere R. v Scunthorpe U.

Tuesday, September 23 1975

DIVISION ONE

Birmingham C. v Newcastle U.
Coventry C. v Middlesbrough
Ipswich T. v Norwich C.
Leeds U. v West Ham U.
Liverpool v Arsenal
Q.P.R. v Leicester C.
Sheffield U. v Burnley
Wolverhampton W. v Aston Villa

DIVISION TWO

Bristol R. v Bolton W.
Fulham v Southampton
Hull C. v Notts Co.
Oldham Ath. v Bristol C.
Orient v York C.
Portsmouth v Chelsea
Sunderland v Carlisle U.

DIVISION THREE

Bury v Mansfield T.
Crystal Palace v Brighton & H.A.
Gillingham v Rotherham U.
Grimsby T. v Halifax T.
Walsall v Shrewsbury T.

DIVISION FOUR

Barnsley v Doncaster R.
Cambridge U. v Watford
Northampton T. v Workington
Southport v Lincoln C.
Swansea C. v Newport Co.

Wednesday, September 24 1975

DIVISION ONE

Derby Co. v Manchester U.
Manchester C. v Stoke C.
Tottenham H. v Everton

DIVISION TWO

Blackburn R. v Blackpool
Luton T. v Plymouth Arg.
Nottingham F. v Charlton Ath.
Oxford U. v W.B.A.

DIVISION THREE

Aldershot v Millwall
Chester v Colchester U.
Chesterfield v Sheffield W.
Hereford U. v Swindon T.
Peterborough U. v Wrexham

DIVISION FOUR

AFC Bournemouth v Brentford
Bradford C. v Huddersfield T.
Crewe Alex. v Rochdale
Hartlepool v Reading
Torquay U. v Exeter C.

Friday, September 26 1975

DIVISION TWO

Charlton Ath. v Hull C.
Orient v Bristol R.

Saturday, September 27 1975

DIVISION ONE

Aston Villa v Birmingham C.
Burnley v Leeds U.
Everton v Liverpool
Ipswich T. v Middlesbrough
Leicester C. v Coventry C.
Manchester C. v Manchester U.
Q.P.R. v Newcastle U.
Sheffield U. v Norwich C.
Stoke C. v Derby Co.
Tottenham H. v Arsenal
Wolverhampton W. v West Ham U.

DIVISION TWO

Bristol C. v Blackpool
Carlisle U. v W.B.A.
Fulham v Chelsea
Luton T. v Blackburn R.
Nottingham F. v Bolton W.
Oldham Ath. v Plymouth Arg.
Southampton v Portsmouth
Sunderland v Notts Co.
York C. v Oxford U.

DIVISION THREE
Brighton & H.A. v Chesterfield
Bury v Millwall
Crystal Palace v Sheffield W.
Grimsby T. v Aldershot
Halifax T. v Chester
Hereford U. v Gillingham
Mansfield T. v Walsall
Peterborough U. v Rotherham U.
Preston N.E. v Cardiff C.
Southend U. v Shrewsbury T.
Swindon T. v Colchester U.
Wrexham v Port Vale

DIVISION FOUR
Barnsley v Workington
Bradford C. v Watford
Darlington v Lincoln C.
Doncaster R. v Southport
Exeter C. v Crewe Alex.
Hartlepool v Tranmere R.
Huddersfield T. v Brentford
Newport Co. v Cambridge U.
Reading v AFC Bournemouth
Stockport Co. v Rochdale
Swansea C. v Scunthorpe U.
Torquay U. v Northampton T.

Friday, October 3 1975
DIVISION TWO
Notts Co. v Bristol C.

Saturday, October 4 1975
DIVISION ONE
Arsenal v Manchester C.
Birmingham C. v Sheffield U.
Coventry C. v Burnley
Derby Co. v Ipswich T.
Leeds U. v Q.P.R.
Liverpool v Wolverhampton W.
Manchester U. v Leicester C.
Middlesbrough v Aston Villa
Newcastle U. v Tottenham H.
Norwich C. v Stoke C.
West Ham U. v Everton

DIVISION TWO
Blackburn R. v Fulham
Blackpool v Luton T.
Bolton W. v Charlton Ath.
Bristol R. v Nottingham F.
Chelsea v York C.
Hull C. v Southampton
Oxford U. v Orient
Plymouth Arg. v Carlisle
Portsmouth v Sunderland
W.B.A. v Oldham Ath.

DIVISION THREE
Aldershot v Southend U.
Cardiff C. v Wrexham
Chester v Hereford U.
Chesterfield v Preston N.E.
Colchester U. v Bury
Gillingham v Halifax T.
Millwall v Mansfield T.
Port Vale v Crystal Palace
Rotherham U. v Swindon T.
Sheffield W. v Peterborough U.
Shrewsbury T. v Brighton & H.A.
Walsall v Grimsby T.

DIVISION FOUR
AFC Bournemouth v Barnsley
Brentford v Newport Co.
Cambridge U. v Darlington
Crewe Alex. v Hartlepool
Lincoln C. v Swansea C.
Northampton T. v Doncaster R.
Rochdale v Exeter C.
Scunthorpe U. v Reading
Southport v Bradford C.
Tranmere R. v Torquay U.
Watford v Stockport Co.
Workington v Huddersfield T.

Friday, October 10 1975
DIVISION THREE
Chesterfield v Shrewsbury T.

DIVISION FOUR
Watford v Workington

Saturday, October 11 1975
DIVISION ONE
Arsenal v Coventry C.
Aston Villa v Tottenham H.
Leeds U. v Manchester U.
Leicester C. v Middlesbrough
Liverpool v Birmingham C.
Manchester C. v Burnley
Norwich C. v Derby Co.
Q.P.R. v Everton
Stoke C. v Ipswich T.
West Ham U. v Newcastle U.
Wolverhampton W. v Sheffield U.

DIVISION TWO
Blackburn R. v W.B.A.
Blackpool v Portsmouth
Bristol C. v Charlton Ath.
Carlisle U. v Luton T.
Fulham v Nottingham F.
Hull C. v Bristol R.
Notts Co. v Oxford U.
Oldham Ath. v York C.
Plymouth Arg. v Bolton W.
Southampton v Chelsea
Sunderland v Orient

DIVISION THREE
Brighton & H.A. v Preston N.E.
Bury v Southend U.
Chester v Aldershot

Colchester U. v Walsall
Crystal Palace v Grimsby T.
Gillingham v Port Vale
Hereford U. v Wrexham
Mansfield T. v Peterborough U.
Rotherham U. v Cardiff C.
Sheffield W. v Millwall
Swindon T. v Halifax T.

DIVISION FOUR
Cambridge U. v Crewe Alex.
Darlington v Exeter C.
Hartlepool v Torquay U.
Lincoln C. v Brentford
Newport Co. v Barnsley
Reading v Bradford C.
Scunthorpe U. v Rochdale
Southport v AFC Bournemouth
Stockport Co. v Doncaster R.
Swansea C. v Huddersfield T.
Tranmere R. v Northampton T.

Friday, October 17 1975
DIVISION FOUR
Barnsley v Reading
Rochdale v Watford

Saturday, October 18 1975
DIVISION ONE
Birmingham C. v Leeds U.
Burnley v Q.P.R.
Coventry C. v Liverpool
Derby Co. v Wolverhampton W.
Everton v Aston Villa
Ipswich T. v Leicester C.
Manchester U. v Arsenal
Middlesbrough v West Ham U.
Newcastle U. v Norwich C.
Sheffield U. v Stoke C.
Tottenham H. v Manchester C.

DIVISION TWO
Bolton W. v Notts Co.
Bristol R. v Sunderland
Charlton Ath. v Oldham Ath.
Chelsea v Blackpool
Luton T. v Fulham
Nottingham F. v Southampton
Orient v Carlisle U.
Oxford U. v Blackburn R.
Portsmouth v Hull C.
W.B.A. v Plymouth Arg.
York C. v Bristol C.

DIVISION THREE
Aldershot v Colchester U.
Cardiff C. v Sheffield W.
Grimsby T. v Brighton & H.A.
Halifax T. v Hereford U.
Millwall v Rotherham U.
Peterborough U. v Bury
Port Vale v Chesterfield
Preston N.E. v Crystal Palace
Shrewsbury T. v Gillingham
Southend U. v Mansfield T.
Walsall v Chester
Wrexham v Swindon T.

DIVISION FOUR
AFC Bournemouth v Tranmere R.
Bradford C. v Stockport Co.
Brentford v Southport
Crewe Alex. v Scunthorpe U.
Doncaster R. v Swansea C.
Exeter C. v Hartlepool
Huddersfield T. v Newport Co.
Northampton T. v Lincoln C.
Rochdale v Watford
Torquay U. v Darlington
Workington v Cambridge U.

Monday, October 20 1975
DIVISION THREE
Mansfield T. v Brighton & H.A.
Southend U. v Halifax T.

DIVISION FOUR
Newport Co. v Reading
Tranmere R. v Southport

Tuesday, October 21 1975
DIVISION TWO
Oldham Ath. v Southampton
Plymouth Arg. v Blackburn R.
Portsmouth v Bristol R.
York C. v Charlton Ath.

DIVISION THREE
Bury v Swindon T.
Colchester U. v Rotherham U.
Crystal Palace v Hereford U.
Gillingham v Chesterfield
Grimsby T. v Wrexham
Preston N.E. v Peterborough U.
Shrewsbury T. v Port Vale
Walsall v Millwall

DIVISION FOUR
Barnsley v Exeter C.
Cambridge U. v Lincoln C.
Huddersfield T. v Torquay U.
Northampton T. v Brentford
Swansea C. v Darlington
Watford v Scunthorpe U.

Wednesday, October 22 1975
DIVISION TWO
Nottingham F. v Luton T.

DIVISION THREE
Aldershot v Cardiff C.
Chester v Sheffield W.

DIVISION FOUR
AFC Bournemouth v Rochdale
Bradford C. v Doncaster R.

Hartlepool v Stockport Co.
Workington v Crewe Alex.

Friday, October 24 1975
DIVISION THREE
Chesterfield v Millwall

DIVISION FOUR
Watford v Crewe Alex.

Saturday, October 25 1975
DIVISION ONE
Arsenal v Middlesbrough
Aston Villa v Burnley
Leeds U. v Coventry C.
Leicester C. v Tottenham H.
Liverpool v Derby Co.
Manchester C. v Ipswich T.
Norwich C. v Birmingham C.
Q.P.R. v Sheffield U.
Stoke C. v Newcastle U.
West Ham U. v Manchester U.
Wolverhampton W. v Everton

DIVISION TWO
Blackburn R. v Chelsea
Blackpool v Bristol R.
Bristol C. v W.B.A.
Carlisle U. v Charlton Ath.
Fulham v Orient
Hull C. v Bolton W.
Notts Co. v Portsmouth
Oldham Ath. v Nottingham F.
Plymouth Arg. v Oxford U.
Southampton v York C.
Sunderland v Luton T.

DIVISION THREE
Brighton & H.A. v Wrexham
Bury v Halifax T.
Chester v Cardiff C.
Colchester U. v Port Vale
Crystal Palace v Southend U.
Gillingham v Walsall
Hereford U. v Peterborough U.
Mansfield T. v Preston N.E.
Rotherham U. v Aldershot
Sheffield W. v Shrewsbury T.
Swindon T. v Grimsby T.

DIVISION FOUR
Cambridge U. v Brentford
Darlington v Doncaster R.
Hartlepool v Barnsley
Lincoln C. v AFC Bournemouth
Newport Co. v Exeter C.
Reading v Huddersfield T.
Scunthorpe U. v Northampton T
Southport v Rochdale
Stockport Co. v Torquay U.
Swansea C. v Bradford C.
Tranmere R. v Workington

Friday, October 31 1975
DIVISION TWO
Charlton Ath. v Southampton

DIVISION THREE
Cardiff C. v Chesterfield

DIVISION FOUR
Barnsley v Swansea C.
Exeter C. v Stockport Co.

Saturday, November 1 1975
DIVISION ONE
Birmingham C. v West Ham U.
Burnley v Stoke C.
Coventry C. v Q.P.R.
Derby Co. v Leeds U.
Everton v Leicester C.
Ipswich T. v Aston Villa
Manchester U. v Norwich C.
Middlesbrough v Liverpool
Newcastle U. v Arsenal
Sheffield U. v Manchester C.
Tottenham H. v Wolverhampton W.

DIVISION TWO
Bolton W. v Blackpool
Bristol R. v Blackburn R.
Chelsea v Plymouth Arg.
Luton T. v Bristol C.
Nottingham F. v Carlisle U.
Orient v Oldham Ath.
Oxford U. v Hull C.
Portsmouth v Fulham
W.B.A. v Notts Co.
York C. v Sunderland

DIVISION THREE
Aldershot v Gillingham
Grimsby T. v Bury
Halifax T. v Crystal Palace
Millwall v Colchester U.
Peterborough U. v Brighton & H.A.
Port Vale v Rotherham U.
Preston N.E. v Hereford U.
Shrewsbury T. v Chester
Southend U. v Swindon T.
Walsall v Sheffield W.
Wrexham v Mansfield T.

DIVISION FOUR
AFC Bournemouth v Cambridge U.
Bradford C. v Darlington
Brentford v Scunthorpe U.
Crewe Alex. v Lincoln C.
Doncaster R. v Reading
Huddersfield T. v Hartlepool
Northampton T. v Watford
Rochdale v Tranmere R.
Torquay U. v Newport Co.
Workington v Southport

Monday, November 3 1975
DIVISION THREE
Port Vale v Aldershot
Wrexham v Southend U.

DIVISION FOUR
Brentford v Workington
Darlington v Hartlepool
Rochdale v Northampton T.
Stockport Co. v Newport Co.

Tuesday, November 4 1975
DIVISION TWO
Blackpool v Nottingham F.
Bolton W. v Portsmouth
Bristol R. v W.B.A.
Carlisle U. v Oldham Ath.
Notts Co. v Plymouth Arg.

DIVISION THREE
Halifax T. v Preston N.E.
Rotherham U. v Chester
Swindon T. v Crystal Palace

DIVISION FOUR
Doncaster R. v Huddersfield T.
Scunthorpe U. v Cambridge U.
Southport v Watford

Wednesday, November 5 1975
DIVISION TWO
Blackburn R. v Hull C.

DIVISION THREE
Brighton & H.A. v Bury
Cardiff C. v Walsall
Chesterfield v Colchester U.
Hereford U. v Mansfield T.
Millwall v Shrewsbury T.
Peterborough U. v Grimsby T.
Sheffield W. v Gillingham

DIVISION FOUR
Crewe Alex. v AFC Bournemouth
Exeter C. v Bradford C.
Lincoln C. v Tranmere R.
Reading v Swansea C.
Torquay U. v Barnsley

Friday, November 7 1975
DIVISION THREE
Chesterfield v Aldershot

DIVISION FOUR
Watford v AFC Bournemouth

Saturday, November 8 1975
DIVISION ONE
Arsenal v Derby Co.
Aston Villa v Sheffield U.
Leeds U. v Newcastle U.
Leicester C. v Burnley
Liverpool v Manchester U.
Manchester C. v Birmingham C.
Norwich C. v Middlesbrough
Q.P.R. v Tottenham H.
Stoke C. v Everton
West Ham U. v Coventry C.
Wolverhampton W. v Ipswich T.

DIVISION TWO
Blackburn R. v Bolton W.
Blackpool v W.B.A.
Bristol C. v Orient
Carlisle U. v York C.
Fulham v Charlton Ath.
Hull C. v Chelsea
Notts Co. v Bristol R.
Oldham Ath. v Oxford U.
Plymouth Arg. v Portsmouth
Southampton v Luton T.
Sunderland v Nottingham F.

DIVISION THREE
Brighton & H.A. v Southend U.
Bury v Wrexham
Chester v Millwall
Colchester U. v Shrewsbury T.
Crystal Palace v Peterborough U.
Gillingham v Cardiff C.
Hereford U. v Grimsby T.
Mansfield T. v Halifax T.
Rotherham U. v Walsall
Sheffield W. v Port Vale
Swindon T. v Preston N.E.

DIVISION FOUR
Cambridge U. v Northampton T.
Darlington v Barnsley
Hartlepool v Doncaster R.
Lincoln C. v Rochdale
Newport Co. v Bradford C.
Reading v Exeter C.
Scunthorpe U. v Workington
Southport v Crewe Alex.
Stockport Co. v Huddersfield T.
Swansea C. v Torquay U.
Tranmere R. v Brentford

Friday, November 14 1975
DIVISION TWO
Orient v Southampton

DIVISION FOUR
Exeter C. v Swansea C.
Rochdale v Cambridge U.

Saturday, November 15 1975
DIVISION ONE
Birmingham C. v Arsenal
Burnley v Wolverhampton W.
Coventry C. v Norwich C.
Derby Co. v West Ham U.
Everton v Manchester C.

Ipswich T. v Q.P.R.
Manchester U. v Aston Villa
Middlesbrough v Leeds U.
Newcastle U. v Liverpool
Sheffield U. v Leicester C.
Tottenham H. v Stoke C.

DIVISION TWO
Bolton W. v Carlisle U.
Bristol R. v Plymouth Arg.
Charlton Ath. v Sunderland
Chelsea v Notts Co.
Luton T. v Oldham Ath.
Nottingham F. v Bristol C.
Oxford U. v Blackpool
Portsmouth v Blackburn R.
W.B.A. v Hull C.
York C. v Fulham

DIVISION THREE
Aldershot v Sheffield W.
Cardiff C. v Colchester U.
Grimsby T. v Mansfield T.
Halifax T. v Brighton & H.A.
Millwall v Gillingham
Peterborough U. v Swindon T.
Port Vale v Chester
Preston N.E. v Bury
Shrewsbury T. v Rotherham U.
Southend U. v Hereford U.
Walsall v Chesterfield
Wrexham v Crystal Palace

DIVISION FOUR
Barnsley v Stockport Co.
AFC Bournemouth v Scunthorpe U.
Bradford C. v Hartlepool
Brentford v Watford
Crewe Alex. v Tranmere R.
Doncaster R. v Newport Co.
Huddersfield T. v Darlington
Northampton T. v Southport
Torquay U. v Reading
Workington v Lincoln C.

Saturday, November 22 1975
DIVISION ONE
Arsenal v Manchester U.
Aston Villa v Everton
Leeds U. v Birmingham C.
Leicester C. v Ipswich T.
Liverpool v Coventry C.
Manchester C. v Tottenham H.
Norwich C. v Newcastle U.
Q.P.R. v Burnley
Stoke C. v Sheffield U.
West Ham U. v Middlesbrough
Wolverhampton W. v Derby Co.

DIVISION TWO
Blackburn R. v Oxford U.
Blackpool v Chelsea
Bristol C. v York C.
Carlisle U. v Orient
Fulham v Luton T.
Hull C. v Portsmouth
Notts Co. v Bolton W.
Oldham Ath. v Charlton Ath.
Plymouth Arg. v W.B.A.
Southampton v Nottingham F.
Sunderland v Bristol R.

Friday, November 28 1975
DIVISION FOUR
Barnsley v Huddersfield T.
Exeter v Doncaster R.
Lincoln C. v Scunthorpe U.
Stockport Co. v Swansea C.

Saturday, November 29 1975
DIVISION ONE
Aston Villa v Leicester C.
Coventry C. v Birmingham C.
Derby Co. v Middlesbrough
Ipswich T. v Sheffield U.
Leeds U. v Everton
Liverpool v Norwich C.
Manchester U. v Newcastle U.
Q.P.R. v Stoke C.
Tottenham H. v Burnley
West Ham U. v Arsenal
Wolverhampton W. v Manchester C.

DIVISION TWO
Blackburn R. v Charlton Ath.
Blackpool v Notts Co.
Bolton W. v W.B.A.
Bristol R. v Chelsea
Carlisle U. v Southampton
Fulham v Bristol C.
Hull C. v Plymouth Arg.
Luton T. v Orient
Nottingham F. v York C.
Portsmouth v Oxford U.
Sunderland v Oldham Ath.

DIVISION THREE
Aldershot v Walsall
Cardiff C. v Shrewsbury T.
Chesterfield v Chester
Crystal Palace v Mansfield T.
Gillingham v Colchester U.
Grimsby T. v Preston N.E.
Hereford U. v Bury
Peterborough U. v Southend U.
Port Vale v Millwall
Sheffield W. v Rotherham U.
Swindon T. v Brighton & H.A.
Wrexham v Halifax T.

DIVISION FOUR
AFC Bournemouth v Northampton T.
Crewe Alex. v Brentford
Darlington v Reading

Hartlepool v Newport Co.
Rochdale v Workington
Southport v Cambridge U.
Torquay U. v Bradford C.
Tranmere R. v Watford

Friday, December 5 1975
DIVISION TWO
Charlton Ath. v Luton T.

DIVISION THREE
Rotherham U v Chesterfield

DIVISION FOUR
Northampton T. v Crewe Alex.

Saturday, December 6 1975
DIVISION ONE
Arsenal v Leeds U.
Birmingham C. v Derby Co.
Burnley v Liverpool
Everton v Ipswich T.
Leicester C. v Wolverhampton W.
Manchester C. v Q.P.R.
Middlesbrough v Manchester U.
Newcastle U. v Coventry C.
Norwich C. v West Ham U.
Sheffield U. v Tottenham H.
Stoke C. v Aston Villa

DIVISION TWO
Bristol C. v Carlisle U.
Chelsea v Bolton W.
Notts Co. v Blackburn R.
Oldham Ath. v Fulham
Orient v Nottingham F.
Oxford U. v Bristol R.
Plymouth Arg. v Blackpool
Southampton v Sunderland
W.B.A. v Portsmouth
York C. v Hull C.

DIVISION THREE
Brighton & H.A. v Hereford U.
Bury v Crystal Palace
Chester v Gillingham
Colchester U. v Sheffield W.
Halifax T. v Peterborough U.
Mansfield T. v Swindon T.
Millwall v Cardiff C.
Preston N.E. v Wrexham
Shrewsbury T. v Aldershot
Southend U. v Grimsby T.
Walsall v Port Vale

DIVISION FOUR
Bradford C. v Barnsley
Brentford v Rochdale
Cambridge U. v Tranmere R.
Doncaster R. v Torquay U.
Huddersfield T. v Exeter C.
Newport Co. v Darlington

Reading v Stockport Co.
Scunthorpe U. v Southport
Swansea C. v Hartlepool
Watford v Lincoln C.
Workington v AFC Bournemouth

Friday, December 12 1975
DIVISION TWO
Orient v Blackpool

Saturday, December 13 1975
DIVISION ONE
Aston Villa v Norwich C.
Burnley v West Ham U.
Everton v Birmingham C.
Ipswich T. v Leeds U.
Leicester C. v Newcastle U.
Manchester C. v Coventry C.
Q.P.R. v Derby Co.
Sheffield U. v Manchester U.
Stoke C. v Arsenal
Tottenham H. v Liverpool
Wolverhampton W. v Middlesbrough

DIVISION TWO
Bristol C. v Hull C.
Carlisle U. v Chelsea
Charlton Ath. v Plymouth Arg.
Fulham v Bolton W.
Luton T. v W.B.A.
Nottingham F. v Portsmouth
Oldham Ath. v Blackburn R.
Southampton v Notts Co.
Sunderland v Oxford U.
York C. v Bristol R.

Friday, December 19 1975
DIVISION THREE
Cardiff C. v Southend U.

Saturday, December 20 1975
DIVISION ONE
Arsenal v Burnley
Birmingham C. v Leicester C.
Coventry C. v Everton
Derby Co. v Sheffield U.
Leeds U. v Aston Villa
Liverpool v Q.P.R.
Manchester U. v Wolverhampton W.
Middlesbrough v Tottenham H.
Newcastle U. v Ipswich T.
Norwich C. v Manchester C.
West Ham U. v Stoke C.

DIVISION TWO
Blackburn R. v Orient
Blackpool v Fulham
Bolton W. v Bristol C.
Bristol R. v Oldham Ath.
Chelsea v Sunderland
Hull C. v Luton T.
Notts Co. v Charlton Ath.

Oxford U. v Carlisle U.
Plymouth Arg. v Nottingham F.
Portsmouth v York C.
W.B.A. v Southampton

DIVISION THREE
Aldershot v Hereford U.
Chester v Swindon T.
Chesterfield v Halifax T.
Colchester U. v Wrexham
Gillingham v Peterborough U
Millwall v Crystal Palace
Port Vale v Grimsby T.
Rotherham U. v Mansfield T.
Sheffield W. v Preston N.E.
Shrewsbury T. v Bury
Walsall v Brighton & H.A.

DIVISION FOUR
AFC Bournemouth v Huddersfield T.
Brentford v Darlington
Cambridge U. v Barnsley
Crewe Alex. v Swansea C.
Lincoln C. v Bradford C.
Northampton T. v Exeter C.
Rochdale v Hartlepool
Scunthorpe U. v Stockport Co.
Southport v Torquay U.
Tranmere R. v Reading
Watford v Newport Co.
Workington v Doncaster R.

Friday, December 26 1975
DIVISION ONE
Aston Villa v West Ham U.
Burnley v Newcastle U.
Everton v Manchester U.
Ipswich T. v Arsenal
Leicester C. v Derby Co.
Manchester C. v Leeds U.
Q.P.R. v Norwich C.
Sheffield U. v Middlesbrough
Stoke C. v Liverpool
Tottenham H. v Birmingham C.
Wolverhampton W. v Coventry C.

DIVISION TWO
Bristol C. v Plymouth Arg.
Carlisle U. v Blackpool
Charlton Ath. v Portsmouth
Fulham v Notts Co.
Luton T. v Oxford U.
Nottingham F. v W.B.A.
Oldham Ath. v Bolton W.
Orient v Chelsea
Southampton v Bristol R.
Sunderland v Hull C.
York C. v Blackburn R.

DIVISION THREE
Brighton & H.A. v Aldershot
Bury v Sheffield W.
Crystal Palace v Gillingham
Grimsby T. v Rotherham U.
Halifax T. v Port Vale
Hereford U. v Walsall
Mansfield T. v Chesterfield
Peterborough U. v Millwall
Preston N.E. v Shrewsbury T.
Southend U. v Colchester U.
Swindon T. v Cardiff C.
Wrexham v Chester

DIVISION FOUR
Barnsley v Rochdale
Bradford C. v Scunthorpe U.
Darlington v Workington
Doncaster R. v Lincoln C.
Exeter C. v Brentford
Hartlepool v Northampton T.
Huddersfield T. v Tranmere R.
Newport Co. v Crewe Alex.
Reading v Cambridge U.
Stockport Co. v Southport
Swansea C. v Watford
Torquay U. v AFC Bournemouth

Saturday, December 27 1975
DIVISION ONE
Arsenal v Q.P.R.
Birmingham C. v Stoke C.
Coventry C. v Tottenham H.
Derby Co. v Aston Villa
Leeds U. v Leicester C.
Liverpool v Manchester C.
Manchester U. v Burnley
Middlesbrough v Everton
Newcastle U. v Sheffield U.
Norwich C. v Wolverhampton W.
West Ham U. v Ipswich T.

DIVISION TWO
Blackburn R. v Nottingham F.
Blackpool v York C.
Bolton W v Sunderland
Bristol R. v Luton T.
Chelsea v Charlton Ath.
Hull C. v Carlisle U.
Notts Co. v Oldham Ath.
Oxford U. v Southampton
Plymouth Arg. v Fulham
Portsmouth v Bristol C.
W.B.A. v Orient

DIVISION THREE
Aldershot v Crystal Palace
Cardiff C. v Peterborough U.
Chester v Preston N.E.
Chesterfield v Southend U.
Colchester U. v Grimsby T.
Gillingham v Brighton & H.A.
Millwall v Swindon T.
Port Vale v Bury
Rotherham U. v Halifax T.

Sheffield W. v Mansfield T.
Shrewsbury T. v Hereford U.
Walsall v Wrexham

DIVISION FOUR
AFC Bournemouth v Swansea C.
Brentford v Reading
Cambridge U. v Torquay U.
Crewe Alex. v Bradford C.
Lincoln C. v Barnsley
Northampton T. v Newport Co.
Rochdale v Darlington
Scunthorpe U. v Doncaster R.
Southport v Huddersfield T.
Tranmere R. v Stockport Co.
Watford v Exeter C.
Workington v Hartlepool

Friday, January 2 1976
DIVISION FOUR
Exeter C. v AFC Bournemouth

Saturday, January 3 1976
DIVISION THREE
Brighton & H.A. v Millwall
Bury v Chester
Crystal Palace v Walsall
Grimsby T. v Chesterfield
Halifax T. v Sheffield W.
Hereford U. v Cardiff C.
Mansfield T. v Port Vale
Peterborough U. v Colchester U.
Preston N.E. v Rotherham U.
Southend U. v Gillingham
Swindon T. v Aldershot
Wrexham v Shrewsbury T.

DIVISION FOUR
Barnsley v Scunthorpe U.
Bradford C. v Workington
Darlington v Southport
Doncaster R. v Rochdale
Hartlepool v Cambridge U.
Huddersfield T. v Crewe Alex.
Newport Co. v Tranmere R.
Reading v Northampton T.
Stockport Co. v Lincoln C.
Swansea C. v Brentford
Torquay U. v Watford

Saturday, January 10 1976
DIVISION ONE
Arsenal v Aston Villa
Birmingham C. v Wolverhampton W.
Coventry C. v Sheffield U.
Derby Co. v Tottenham H.
Leeds U. v Stoke C.
Liverpool v Ipswich T.
Manchester U. v Q.P.R.
Middlesbrough v Manchester C.
Newcastle U. v Everton
Norwich C. v Burnley
West Ham U. v Leicester C.

DIVISION TWO
Blackburn R. v Southampton
Blackpool v Charlton Ath.
Bolton W. v Luton T.
Bristol R. v Fulham
Chelsea v Oldham Ath.
Hull C. v Nottingham F.
Notts Co. v York C.
Oxford U. v Bristol C.
Plymouth Arg. v Orient
Portsmouth v Carlisle U.
W.B.A. v Sunderland

DIVISION THREE
Aldershot v Bury
Cardiff C. v Brighton & H.A.
Chester v Mansfield T.
Chesterfield v Wrexham
Colchester U. v Crystal Palace
Gillingham v Swindon T.
Mansfield T. v Preston N.E.
Port Vale v Peterborough U.
Rotherham U. v Southend U.
Sheffield W. v Hereford U.
Shrewsbury T. v Grimsby T.
Walsall v Halifax T.

DIVISION FOUR
AFC Bournemouth v Bradford C.
Brentford v Torquay U.
Cambridge U. v Swansea C.
Crewe Alex. v Doncaster R.
Lincoln C. v Hartlepool
Northampton T. v Barnsley
Rochdale v Huddersfield T.
Scunthorpe U. v Newport Co.
Southport v Reading
Tranmere R. v Exeter C.
Watford v Darlington
Workington v Stockport Co.

Friday, January 16 1976
DIVISION TWO
Orient v Hull C.

DIVISION FOUR
Barnsley v Tranmere R.
Swansea C. v Northampton T.

Saturday, January 17 1976
DIVISION ONE
Aston Villa v Newcastle U.
Burnley v Derby Co.
Everton v Norwich C.
Ipswich T. v Coventry C.
Leicester C. v Arsenal
Manchester C. v West Ham U.
Q.P.R. v Birmingham C.
Sheffield U. v Liverpool
Stoke C. v Middlesbrough
Tottenham H. v Manchester U.
Wolverhampton W. v Leeds U.

DIVISION TWO
Bristol C. v Blackburn R.
Carlisle U. v Notts Co.
Charlton Ath. v Bristol R.
Fulham v Oxford U.
Luton T. v Portsmouth
Nottingham F. v Chelsea
Oldham Ath. v Blackpool
Southampton v Bolton W.
Sunderland v Plymouth Arg.
York C. v W.B.A.

DIVISION THREE
Brighton & H.A. v Colchester U.
Bury v Walsall
Crystal Palace v Shrewsbury T.
Grimsby T. v Sheffield W.
Halifax T. v Cardiff C.
Hereford U. v Chesterfield
Mansfield T. v Gillingham
Peterborough U. v Chester
Preston N.E. v Aldershot
Southend U. v Millwall
Swindon T. v Port Vale
Wrexham v Rotherham U.

DIVISION FOUR
Bradford C. v Rochdale
Darlington v Crewe Alex.
Doncaster R. v Watford
Exeter C. v Lincoln C.
Hartlepool v Southport
Huddersfield T. v Cambridge U.
Newport Co. v AFC Bournemouth
Reading v Workington
Stockport Co. v Brentford
Torquay U. v Scunthorpe U.

Friday, January 23 1976
DIVISION THREE
Cardiff C. v Mansfield T.

Saturday, January 24 1976
DIVISION THREE
Aldershot v Peterborough U.
Chester v Brighton & H.A.
Chesterfield v Bury
Colchester U. v Hereford U.
Gillingham v Wrexham
Millwall v Grimsby T.
Port Vale v Southend U.
Rotherham U. v Crystal Palace
Sheffield W. v Swindon T.
Shrewsbury T. v Halifax T.
Walsall v Preston N.E.

DIVISION FOUR
AFC Bournemouth v Stockport Co.
Brentford v Doncaster R.
Cambridge U. v Exeter C.
Crewe Alex. v Barnsley
Lincoln C. v Huddersfield T.
Northampton T. v Darlington
Rochdale v Torquay U.
Scunthorpe U. v Hartlepool
Southport v Newport Co.
Tranmere R. v Bradford C.
Watford v Reading
Workington v Swansea C.

Friday, January 30 1976
DIVISION TWO
Sunderland v Bristol C.

DIVISION THREE
Halifax T. v Southend U.

DIVISION FOUR
Doncaster R. v Bradford C.
Stockport Co. v Hartlepool

Saturday, January 31 1976
DIVISION ONE
Arsenal v Sheffield U.
Aston Villa v Q.P.R.
Derby Co. v Coventry C.
Everton v Burnley
Ipswich T. v Tottenham H.
Leeds U. v Norwich C.
Leicester C. v Manchester C.
Manchester U. v Birmingham C.
Middlesbrough v Newcastle U.
West Ham U. v Liverpool
Wolverhampton W. v Stoke C.

DIVISION TWO
Blackburn R. v Plymouth Arg.
Blackpool v Hull C.
Bolton W. v Oxford U.
Bristol R. v Portsmouth
Carlisle U. v Fulham
Charlton Ath. v York C.
Chelsea v W.B.A.
Luton T. v Nottingham F.
Notts Co. v Orient
Southampton v Oldham Ath.
Sunderland v Bristol C.

DIVISION THREE
Brighton & H.A. v Mansfield T.
Cardiff C. v Aldershot
Chesterfield v Gillingham
Hereford U. v Crystal Palace
Millwall v Walsall
Peterborough U. v Preston N.E.
Port Vale v Shrewsbury T.
Rotherham U. v Colchester U.
Sheffield W. v Chester
Swindon T. v Bury
Wrexham v Grimsby T.

DIVISION FOUR
Brentford v Northampton T.
Crewe Alex. v Workington
Darlington v Swansea C.

Exeter C. v Barnsley
Lincoln C. v Cambridge U.
Reading v Newport Co.
Rochdale v AFC Bournemouth
Scunthorpe U. v Watford
Southport v Tranmere R.
Torquay U. v Huddersfield T.

Friday, February 6 1976
DIVISION TWO
Hull C. v Blackburn R.
Orient v Charlton Ath.

DIVISION FOUR
Swansea C. v Reading

Saturday, February 7 1976
DIVISION ONE
Birmingham C. v Middlesbrough
Burnley v Ipswich T.
Coventry C. v Manchester U.
Liverpool v Leeds U.
Manchester C. v Aston Villa
Newcastle U. v Derby Co.
Norwich C. v Arsenal
Q.P.R. v Wolverhampton W.
Sheffield U. v Everton
Stoke C. v Leicester C.
Tottenham H. v West Ham U.

DIVISION TWO
Bristol C. v Southampton
Fulham v Sunderland
Nottingham F. v Blackpool
Oldham Ath. v Carlisle U.
Oxford U. v Chelsea
Plymouth Arg. v Notts C.
Portsmouth v Bolton W.
W.B.A. v Bristol R.
York C. v Luton T.

DIVISION THREE
Aldershot v Port Vale
Bury v Brighton & H.A.
Chester v Rotherham U.
Colchester U. v Chesterfield
Crystal Palace v Swindon T.
Gillingham v Sheffield W.
Grimsby T. v Peterborough U.
Mansfield T. v Hereford U.
Preston N.E. v Halifax T.
Shrewsbury T. v Millwall
Southend U. v Wrexham
Walsall v Cardiff C.

DIVISION FOUR
Barnsley v Torquay U.
AFC Bournemouth v Crewe Alex.
Bradford C. v Exeter C.
Cambridge U. v Scunthorpe U.
Hartlepool v Darlington
Huddersfield T. v Doncaster R.

Newport Co. v Stockport Co.
Northampton T. v Rochdale
Tranmere R. v Lincoln C.
Watford v Southport
Workington v Brentford

Friday, February 13 1976
DIVISION TWO
Charlton Ath. v Fulham

DIVISION FOUR
Exeter C. v Reading

Saturday, February 14 1976
DIVISION ONE
Birmingham C. v Manchester C.
Burnley v Leicester C.
Coventry C. v West Ham U.
Derby Co. v Arsenal
Everton v Stoke C.
Ipswich T. v Wolverhampton W.
Manchester U. v Liverpool
Middlesbrough v Norwich C.
Newcastle U. v Leeds U.
Sheffield U. v Aston Villa
Tottenham H. v Q.P.R.

DIVISION TWO
Bolton W. v Blackburn R.
Bristol R. v Notts Co.
Chelsea v Hull C.
Luton T. v Southampton
Nottingham F. v Sunderland
Orient v Bristol C.
Oxford U. v Oldham Ath.
Portsmouth v Plymouth Arg.
W.B.A. v Blackpool
York C. v Carlisle U.

DIVISION THREE
Aldershot v Chesterfield
Cardiff C. v Gillingham
Grimsby T. v Hereford U.
Halifax T. v Mansfield T.
Millwall v Chester
Peterborough U. v Crystal Palace
Port Vale v Sheffield W.
Preston N.E. v Swindon T.
Shrewsbury T. v Colchester U.
Southend U. v Brighton & H.A.
Walsall v Rotherham U.
Wrexham v Bury

DIVISION FOUR
Barnsley v Darlington
AFC Bournemouth v Watford
Bradford C. v Newport Co.
Brentford v Tranmere R.
Crewe Alex. v Southport
Doncaster R. v Hartlepool
Huddersfield T. v Stockport Co.
Northampton T. v Cambridge U.

Rochdale v Lincoln C.
Torquay U. v Swansea C.
Workington v Scunthorpe U.

Friday, February 20 1976
DIVISION THREE
Chesterfield v Walsall

DIVISION FOUR
Watford v Brentford

Saturday, February 21 1976
DIVISION ONE
Arsenal v Birmingham C.
Aston Villa v Manchester U.
Leeds U. v Middlesbrough
Leicester C. v Sheffield U.
Liverpool v Newcastle U.
Manchester C. v Everton
Norwich C. v Coventry C.
Q.P.R. v Ipswich T.
Stoke C. v Tottenham H.
West Ham U. v Derby Co.
Wolverhampton W. v Burnley

DIVISION TWO
Blackburn R. v Portsmouth
Blackpool v Oxford U.
Bristol C. v Nottingham F.
Carlisle U. v Bolton W.
Fulham v York C.
Hull C. v W.B.A.
Notts Co. v Chelsea
Oldham Ath. v Luton T.
Plymouth Arg. v Bristol R.
Southampton v Orient
Sunderland v Charlton Ath.

DIVISION THREE
Brighton & H.A. v Halifax T.
Bury v Preston N.E.
Chester v Port Vale
Colchester U. v Cardiff C.
Crystal Palace v Wrexham
Gillingham v Millwall
Hereford U. v Southend U.
Mansfield T. v Grimsby T.
Rotherham U. v Shrewsbury T.
Sheffield W. v Aldershot
Swindon T. v Peterborough U.

DIVISION FOUR
Cambridge U. v Rochdale
Darlington v Huddersfield T.
Hartlepool v Bradford C.
Lincoln C. v Workington
Newport Co. v Doncaster R.
Reading v Torquay U.
Scunthorpe U. v AFC Bournemouth
Southport v Northampton T.
Stockport Co. v Barnsley
Swansea C. v Exeter C.
Tranmere R. v Crewe Alex.

Monday, February 23 1976
DIVISION ONE
West Ham U. v Leeds U.

DIVISION THREE
Mansfield T. v Bury
Wrexham v Peterborough U.

DIVISION FOUR
Brentford v AFC Bournemouth
Darlington v Stockport Co.
Newport Co. v Swansea C.
Rochdale v Crewe Alex.

Tuesday, February 24 1976
DIVISION ONE
Arsenal v Liverpool
Burnley v Sheffield U.
Everton v Tottenham H.
Middlesbrough v Coventry C.

DIVISION TWO
Blackpool v Blackburn R.
Bolton W. v Bristol R.
Bristol C. v Oldham Ath.
Carlisle U. v Sunderland
Charlton Ath. v Nottingham F.
Notts Co. v Hull C.
Plymouth Arg. v Luton T.
Southampton v Fulham
York C. v Orient

DIVISION THREE
Colchester U. v Chester
Halifax T. v Grimsby T.
Preston N.E. v Southend U.
Rotherham U. v Gillingham
Shrewsbury T. v Walsall
Swindon T. v Hereford U.

DIVISION FOUR
Doncaster R. v Barnsley
Huddersfield T. v Bradford C.
Scunthorpe U. v Tranmere R.
Watford v Cambridge U.

Wednesday, February 25 1976
DIVISION ONE
Aston Villa v Wolverhampton W.
Leicester C. v Q.P.R.
Manchester U. v Derby Co.
Newcastle U. v Birmingham C.
Norwich C. v Ipswich T.
Stoke C. v Manchester C.

DIVISION TWO
Chelsea v Portsmouth
W.B.A. v Oxford U.

DIVISION THREE
Brighton & H.A. v Crystal Palace
Cardiff C. v Port Vale

Millwall v Aldershot
Sheffield W. v Chesterfield

DIVISION FOUR
Exeter C. v Torquay U.
Lincoln C. v Southport
Reading v Hartlepool
Workington v Northampton T.

Saturday, February 28 1976
DIVISION ONE
Birmingham C. v Norwich C.
Burnley v Aston Villa
Coventry C. v Leeds U.
Derby Co. v Liverpool
Everton v Wolverhampton W.
Ipswich T. v Manchester C.
Manchester U. v West Ham U.
Middlesbrough v Arsenal
Newcastle U. v Stoke C.
Sheffield U. v Q.P.R.
Tottenham H. v Leicester C.

DIVISION TWO
Bolton W. v Hull C.
Bristol R. v Blackpool
Charlton Ath. v Carlisle U.
Chelsea v Blackburn R.
Luton T. v Sunderland
Nottingham F. v Oldham Ath.
Orient v Fulham
Oxford U. v Plymouth Arg.
Portsmouth v Notts Co.
W.B.A. v Bristol C.
York C. v Southampton

DIVISION THREE
Aldershot v Rotherham U.
Cardiff C. v Chester
Grimsby T. v Swindon T.
Halifax T. v Bury
Millwall v Chesterfield
Peterborough U. v Hereford U.
Port Vale v Colchester U.
Preston N.E. v Mansfield T.
Shrewsbury T. v Sheffield W.
Southend U. v Crystal Palace
Walsall v Gillingham
Wrexham v Brighton & H.A.

DIVISION FOUR
Barnsley v Hartlepool
AFC Bournemouth v Lincoln C.
Bradford C. v Swansea C.
Brentford v Cambridge U.
Crewe Alex. v Watford
Doncaster R. v Darlington
Exeter C. v Newport Co.
Huddersfield T. v Reading
Northampton T. v Scunthorpe U.
Rochdale v Southport
Torquay U. v Stockport Co.
Workington v Tranmere R.

Friday, March 5 1976
DIVISION THREE
Chesterfield v Cardiff C.

DIVISION FOUR
Swansea C. v Barnsley
Watford v Northampton T.

Saturday, March 6 1976
DIVISION ONE
Arsenal v Newcastle U.
Aston Villa v Ipswich T.
Leeds U. v Derby Co.
Leicester C. v Everton
Liverpool v Middlesbrough
Manchester C. v Sheffield U.
Norwich C. v Manchester U.
Q.P.R. v Coventry C.
Stoke C. v Burnley
West Ham U. v Birmingham C.
Wolverhampton W. v Tottenham H.

DIVISION TWO
Blackburn R. v Bristol R.
Blackpool v Bolton W.
Bristol C. v Luton T.
Carlisle U. v Nottingham F.
Fulham v Portsmouth
Hull C. v Oxford U.
Notts Co. v W.B.A.
Oldham Ath. v Orient
Plymouth Arg. v Chelsea
Southampton v Charlton Ath.
Sunderland v York C.

DIVISION THREE
Brighton & H.A. v Peterborough U.
Bury v Grimsby T.
Chester v Shrewsbury T.
Colchester U. v Millwall
Crystal Palace v Halifax T.
Gillingham v Aldershot
Hereford U. v Preston N.E.
Mansfield T. v Wrexham
Rotherham U. v Port Vale
Sheffield W. v Walsall
Swindon T. v Southend U.

DIVISION FOUR
Cambridge U. v AFC Bournemouth
Darlington v Bradford C.
Hartlepool v Huddersfield T.
Lincoln C. v Crewe Alex.
Newport Co. v Torquay U.
Reading v Doncaster R.
Scunthorpe U. v Brentford
Southport v Workington
Stockport Co. v Exeter C.
Tranmere R. v Rochdale

Monday, March 8 1976
DIVISION THREE
Mansfield T. v Millwall
Southend U. v Aldershot
Wrexham v Cardiff C.

DIVISION FOUR
Darlington v Cambridge U.
Newport Co. v Brentford
Stockport Co. v Watford

Tuesday, March 9 1976
DIVISION THREE
Bury v Colchester U.
Crystal Palace v Port Vale
Grimsby T. v Walsall
Halifax T. v Gillingham
Preston N.E. v Chesterfield
Swindon T. v Rotherham U.

DIVISION FOUR
Barnsley v AFC Bournemouth
Doncaster R. v Northampton T.
Huddersfield T. v Workington
Swansea C. v Lincoln C.

Wednesday, March 10 1976
DIVISION THREE
Brighton & H.A. v Shrewsbury T.
Hereford U. v Chester
Peterborough U. v Sheffield W.

DIVISION FOUR
Bradford C. v Southport
Exeter C. v Rochdale
Hartlepool v Crewe Alex.
Reading v Scunthorpe U.
Torquay U. v Tranmere R.

Friday, March 12 1976
DIVISION TWO
Charlton Ath. v Bristol C.

DIVISION FOUR
Rochdale v Scunthorpe U.

Saturday, March 13 1976
DIVISION ONE
Birmingham C. v Liverpool
Burnley v Manchester C.
Coventry C. v Arsenal
Derby Co. v Norwich C.
Everton v Q.P.R.
Ipswich T. v Stoke C.
Manchester U. v Leeds U.
Middlesbrough v Leicester C.
Newcastle U. v West Ham U.
Sheffield U. v Wolverhampton W.
Tottenham H. v Aston Villa

DIVISION TWO
Bolton W. v Plymouth Arg.
Bristol R. v Hull C.
Chelsea v Southampton
Luton T. v Carlisle U.
Nottingham F. v Fulham
Orient v Sunderland
Oxford U. v Notts Co.
Portsmouth v Blackpool
W.B.A. v Blackburn R.
York C. v Oldham Ath.

DIVISION THREE
Aldershot v Chester
Cardiff C. v Rotherham U.
Grimsby T. v Crystal Palace
Halifax T. v Swindon T.
Millwall v Sheffield W.
Peterborough U. v Mansfield T.
Port Vale v Gillingham
Preston N.E. v Brighton & H.A.
Shrewsbury T. v Chesterfield
Southend U. v Bury
Walsall v Colchester U.
Wrexham v Hereford U.

DIVISION FOUR
Barnsley v Newport Co.
AFC Bournemouth v Southport
Bradford C. v Reading
Brentford v Lincoln C.
Crewe Alex. v Cambridge U.
Doncaster R. v Stockport Co.
Exeter C. v Darlington
Huddersfield T. v Swansea C.
Northampton T. v Tranmere R.
Torquay U. v Hartlepool
Workington v Watford

Monday, March 15 1976
DIVISION THREE
Mansfield T. v Southend U.

DIVISION FOUR
Darlington v Torquay U.
Newport Co. v Huddersfield T.
Stockport Co. v Bradford C.
Tranmere R. v AFC Bournemouth

Tuesday, March 16 1976
DIVISION THREE
Bury v Peterborough U.
Colchester U. v Aldershot
Crystal Palace v Preston N.E.
Gillingham v Shrewsbury T.
Rotherham U. v Millwall
Swindon T. v Wrexham

DIVISION FOUR
Cambridge U. v Workington
Scunthorpe U. v Crewe Alex.
Southport v Brentford
Swansea C. v Doncaster R.
Watford v Rochdale

Wednesday, March 17 1976
DIVISION THREE
Brighton & H.A. v Grimsby T.
Chester v Walsall
Chesterfield v Port Vale

Hereford U. v Halifax T.
Sheffield W. v Cardiff C.

DIVISION FOUR
Hartlepool v Exeter C.
Lincoln C. v Northampton T.
Reading v Barnsley

Friday, March 19 1976
DIVISION THREE
Rotherham U. v Sheffield W.

DIVISION FOUR
Northampton T. v AFC Bournemouth

Saturday, March 20 1976
DIVISION ONE
Arsenal v West Ham U.
Birmingham C. v Coventry C.
Burnley v Tottenham H.
Everton v Leeds U.
Leicester C. v Aston Villa
Manchester C. v Wolverhampton W.
Middlesbrough v Derby Co.
Newcastle U. v Manchester U.
Norwich C. v Liverpool
Sheffield U. v Ipswich T.
Stoke C. v Q.P.R.

DIVISION TWO
Bristol C. v Fulham
Charlton Ath. v Blackburn R.
Chelsea v Bristol R.
Notts Co. v Blackpool
Oldham Ath. v Sunderland
Orient v Luton T.
Oxford U. v Portsmouth
Plymouth Arg. v Hull C.
Southampton v Carlisle U.
W.B.A. v Bolton W.
York C. v Nottingham F.

DIVISION THREE
Brighton & H.A. v Swindon T.
Bury v Hereford U.
Chester v Chesterfield
Colchester U. v Gillingham
Halifax T. v Wrexham
Mansfield T. v Crystal Palace
Millwall v Port Vale
Preston N.E. v Grimsby T.
Shrewsbury T. v Cardiff C.
Southend U. v Peterborough U.
Walsall v Aldershot

DIVISION FOUR
Bradford C. v Torquay U.
Brentford v Crewe Alex.
Cambridge U. v Southport
Doncaster R. v Exeter C.
Huddersfield T. v Barnsley
Newport Co. v Hartlepool
Reading v Darlington
Scunthorpe U. v Lincoln C.
Swansea C. v Stockport Co.
Watford v Tranmere R.
Workington v Rochdale

Friday, March 26 1976
DIVISION FOUR
Barnsley v Bradford C.
Lincoln C. v Watford
Stockport Co. v Reading

Saturday, March 27 1976
DIVISION ONE
Aston Villa v Stoke C.
Coventry C. v Newcastle U.
Derby Co. v Birmingham C.
Ipswich T. v Everton
Leeds U. v Arsenal
Liverpool v Burnley
Manchester U. v Middlesbrough
Q.P.R. v Manchester C.
Tottenham H. v Sheffield U.
West Ham U. v Norwich C.
Wolverhampton W. v Leicester C.

DIVISION TWO
Blackburn R. v Notts Co.
Blackpool v Plymouth Arg.
Bolton W. v Chelsea
Bristol R. v Oxford U.
Carlisle U. v Bristol C.
Fulham v Oldham Ath.
Hull C. v York C.
Luton T. v Charlton Ath.
Nottingham F. v Orient
Portsmouth v W.B.A.
Sunderland v Southampton

DIVISION THREE
Aldershot v Shrewsbury T.
Cardiff C. v Millwall
Chesterfield v Rotherham U.
Crystal Palace v Bury
Gillingham v Chester
Grimsby T. v Southend U.
Hereford U. v Brighton & H.A.
Peterborough U. v Halifax T.
Port Vale v Walsall
Sheffield W. v Colchester U.
Swindon T. v Mansfield T.
Wrexham v Preston N.E.

DIVISION FOUR
AFC Bournemouth v Workington
Crewe Alex. v Northampton T.
Darlington v Newport Co.
Exeter C. v Huddersfield T.
Hartlepool v Swansea C.
Rochdale v Brentford
Southport v Scunthorpe U.
Torquay U. v Doncaster R.
Tranmere R. v Cambridge U.

Monday, March 29 1976
DIVISION THREE
Mansfield T. v Rotherham U.
Southend U. v Cardiff C.
Wrexham v Colchester U.

DIVISION FOUR
Darlington v Brentford
Newport Co. v Watford
Stockport Co. v Scunthorpe U.

Tuesday, March 30 1976
DIVISION THREE
Bury v Shrewsbury T.
Crystal Palace v Millwall
Grimsby T. v Port Vale
Halifax T. v Chesterfield
Preston N.E. v Sheffield W.
Swindon T. v Chester

DIVISION FOUR
Barnsley v Cambridge U.
Doncaster R. v Workington
Huddersfield T. v AFC Bournemouth
Swansea C. v Crewe Alex.

Wednesday, March 31 1976
DIVISION THREE
Brighton & H.A. v Walsall
Hereford U. v Aldershot
Peterborough U. v Gillingham

DIVISION FOUR
Bradford C. v Lincoln C.
Exeter C. v Northampton T.
Hartlepool v Rochdale
Reading v Tranmere R.
Torquay U. v Southport

Saturday, April 3 1976
DIVISION ONE
Arsenal v Tottenham H.
Birmingham C. v Aston Villa
Coventry C. v Leicester C.
Derby Co. v Stoke C.
Leeds U. v Burnley
Liverpool v Everton
Manchester U. v Manchester C.
Middlesbrough v Ipswich T.
Newcastle U. v Q.P.R.
Norwich C. v Sheffield U.
West Ham U. v Wolverhampton W.

DIVISION TWO
Blackburn R. v Luton T.
Blackpool v Bristol C.
Bolton W. v Nottingham F.
Bristol R. v Orient
Chelsea v Fulham
Hull C. v Charlton Ath.
Notts Co. v Sunderland
Oxford U. v York C.
Plymouth Arg. v Oldham Ath.
Portsmouth v Southampton
W.B.A. v Carlisle U

DIVISION THREE
Aldershot v Wrexham
Cardiff C. v Grimsby T.
Chester v Crystal Palace
Chesterfield v Swindon T.
Colchester U. v Preston N.E.
Gillingham v Bury
Millwall v Halifax T.
Port Vale v Hereford U.
Rotherham U. v Brighton & H.A.
Sheffield W. v Southend U.
Shrewsbury T. v Mansfield T.
Walsall v Peterborough U.

DIVISION FOUR
AFC Bournemouth v Hartlepool
Brentford v Bradford C.
Cambridge U. v Doncaster R.
Crewe Alex. v Stockport Co.
Lincoln C. v Newport Co.
Northampton T. v Huddersfield T.
Rochdale v Reading
Scunthorpe U. v Darlington
Southport v Exeter C.
Tranmere R. v Swansea C.
Watford v Barnsley
Workington v Torquay U.

Monday, April 5 1976
DIVISION THREE
Port Vale v Wrexham

DIVISION FOUR
Brentford v Huddersfield T.
Rochdale v Stockport Co.
Tranmere R. v Hartlepool

Tuesday, April 6 1976
DIVISION THREE
Colchester U. v Swindon T.
Gillingham v Hereford U.
Rotherham U. v Peterborough U.
Shrewsbury T. v Southend U.
Walsall v Mansfield T.

DIVISION FOUR
Cambridge U. v Newport Co.
Northampton T. v Torquay U.
Scunthorpe U. v Swansea C.
Southport v Doncaster R.
Watford v Bradford C.

Wednesday, April 7 1976
DIVISION THREE
Aldershot v Grimsby T.
Cardiff C. v Preston N.E.
Chester v Halifax T.
Chesterfield v Brighton & H.A.
Millwall v Bury
Sheffield W. v Crystal Palace

DIVISION FOUR
AFC Bournemouth v Reading
Crewe Alex. v Exeter C.
Lincoln C. v Darlington
Workington v Barnsley

Friday, April 9 1976
DIVISION TWO
Charlton Ath. v W.B.A.
Orient v Bolton W.

Saturday, April 10 1976
DIVISION ONE
Aston Villa v Liverpool
Burnley v Birmingham C.
Everton v Arsenal
Ipswich T. v Manchester U.
Leicester C. v Norwich C.
Manchester C. v Derby C.
Q.P.R. v Middlesbrough
Sheffield U. v West Ham U.
Stoke C. v Coventry C.
Tottenham H. v Leeds U.
Wolverhampton W. v Newcastle U.

DIVISION TWO
Bristol C. v Chelsea
Carlisle U. v Bristol R.
Fulham v Hull C.
Luton T. v Notts Co.
Nottingham F. v Oxford U.
Oldham Ath. v Portsmouth
Southampton v Blackpool
Sunderland v Blackburn R.
York C. v Plymouth Arg.

DIVISION THREE
Brighton & H.A. v Port Vale
Bury v Rotherham U.
Crystal Palace v Cardiff C.
Grimsby T. v Chester
Halifax T. v Colchester U.
Hereford U. v Millwall
Mansfield T. v Aldershot
Peterborough U. v Chesterfield
Preston N.E. v Gillingham
Southend U. v Walsall
Swindon T. v Shrewsbury T.
Wrexham v Sheffield W.

DIVISION FOUR
Barnsley v Brentford
Bradford C. v Northampton T.
Darlington v Tranmere R.
Doncaster R. v AFC Bournemouth
Exeter C. v Workington
Hartlepool v Watford
Huddersfield T. v Scunthorpe U.
Newport Co. v Rochdale
Reading v Lincoln C.
Stockport Co. v Cambridge U.
Swansea C. v Southport
Torquay U. v Crewe Alex.

Friday, April 16 1976
DIVISION ONE
Coventry C. v Aston Villa
Leeds U. v Sheffield U.
Liverpool v Leicester C.
Middlesbrough v Burnley
Newcastle U. v Manchester C.
West Ham U. v Q.P.R.

DIVISION TWO
Blackburn R. v Carlisle U.
Bolton W. v York C.
Bristol R. v Bristol C.
Chelsea v Luton T.
Hull C. v Oldham Ath.
Notts Co. v Nottingham F.
Oxford U. v Charlton Ath.
Plymouth Arg. v Southampton
Portsmouth v Orient
W.B.A. v Fulham

DIVISION THREE
Aldershot v Swindon T.
Cardiff C. v Hereford U.
Chester v Bury
Chesterfield v Grimsby T.
Colchester U. v Peterborough U.
Gillingham v Southend U.
Millwall v Brighton & H.A.
Walsall v Crystal Palace

DIVISION FOUR
AFC Bournemouth v Exeter C.
Brentford v Swansea C.
Cambridge U. v Hartlepool
Crewe Alex. v Huddersfield T.
Lincoln C. v Stockport Co.
Northampton T. v Reading
Rochdale v Doncaster R.
Southport v Darlington
Tranmere R. v Newport Co.
Watford v Torquay U.
Workington v Bradford C.

Saturday, April 17 1976
DIVISION ONE
Arsenal v Ipswich T.
Birmingham C. v Tottenham H.
Coventry C. v Wolverhampton W.
Derby Co. v Leicester C.
Leeds U. v Manchester C.
Liverpool v Stoke C.
Manchester U. v Everton
Middlesbrough v Sheffield U.
Newcastle U. v Burnley
Norwich C. v Q.P.R.
West Ham U. v Aston Villa

DIVISION TWO
Blackburn R. v York C.
Blackpool v Carlisle U.
Bolton W. v Oldham Ath.

Bristol R. v Southampton
Chelsea v Orient
Hull C. v Sunderland
Notts Co. v Fulham
Oxford U. v Luton T.
Plymouth Arg. v Bristol C.
Portsmouth v Charlton Ath.
W.B.A. v Nottingham F.

DIVISION THREE
Aldershot v Brighton & H.A.
Cardiff C. v Swindon T.
Chester v Wrexham
Chesterfield v Mansfield T.
Colchester U. v Southend U.
Gillingham v Crystal Palace
Millwall v Peterborough U.
Port Vale v Halifax T.
Rotherham U. v Grimsby T.
Sheffield W. v Bury
Shrewsbury T. v Preston N.E.
Walsall v Hereford U.

DIVISION FOUR
AFC Bournemouth v Torquay
Brentford v Exeter C.
Cambridge U. v Reading
Crewe Alex. v Newport Co.
Lincoln C. v Doncaster R.
Northampton T. v Hartlepool
Rochdale v Barnsley
Scunthorpe U. v Bradford C.
Southport v Stockport Co.
Tranmere R. v Huddersfield T.
Watford v Swansea C.
Workington v Darlington

Monday, April 19 1976:
DIVISION ONE
Aston Villa v Derby Co.
Burnley v Manchester U.
Everton v Middlesbrough
Ipswich T. v West Ham U.
Leicester C. v Leeds U.
Manchester C. v Liverpool
Q.P.R. v Arsenal
Sheffield U. v Newcastle U.
Stoke C. v Birmingham C.
Tottenham H. v Coventry C.
Wolverhampton W. v Norwich C.

DIVISION TWO
Charlton Ath. v Chelsea
Fulham v Plymouth Arg.
Luton T. v Bristol R.
Oldham Ath. v Notts Co.
Southampton v Oxford U.
Sunderland v Bolton W.
York C. v Blackpool

DIVISION THREE
Brighton & H.A. v Gillingham
Bury v Port Vale
Grimsby T. v Colchester U.
Halifax T. v Rotherham U.
Hereford U. v Shrewsbury T.
Mansfield T. v Sheffield W.
Peterborough U. v Cardiff C.
Preston N. E. v Chester
Southend U. v Chesterfield
Wrexham v Walsall

DIVISION FOUR
Barnsley v Lincoln C.
Bradford C. v Crewe Alex.
Doncaster R. v Scunthorpe U.
Exeter C. v Watford
Huddersfield T. v Southport
Reading v Brentford
Stockport Co. v Tranmere R.
Swansea C. v AFC Bournemouth
Torquay U. v Cambridge U.

Tuesday, April 20 1976
DIVISION ONE
Arsenal v Wolverhampton W.
Birmingham C. v Ipswich T.
Derby Co. v Everton
Manchester U. v Stoke C.
Norwich C. v Tottenham H.

DIVISION TWO
Blackpool v Sunderland
Bristol C. v Portsmouth
Carlisle U. v Hull C.
Nottingham F. v Blackburn R.
Orient v W.B.A.

DIVISION THREE
Crystal Palace v Aldershot
Port Vale v Mansfield T.
Rotherham U. v Preston N.E.
Sheffield W. v Halifax T.
Shrewsbury T. v Wrexham
Swindon T. v Millwall

DIVISION FOUR
Darlington v Rochdale
Hartlepool v Workington
Newport Co. v Northampton T.
Scunthorpe U. v Barnsley

Friday, April 23 1976
DIVISION FOUR
Exeter C. v Scunthorpe U.

Saturday, April 24 1976
DIVISION ONE
Aston Villa v Middlesbrough
Burnley v Coventry C.
Everton v West Ham U.
Ipswich T. v Derby Co.
Leicester C. v Manchester U.
Manchester C. v Arsenal
Q.P.R. v Leeds U.

Sheffield U. v Birmingham C.
Stoke C. v Norwich C.
Tottenham H. v Newcastle U.
Wolverhampton W. v Liverpool

DIVISION TWO
Bristol C. v Notts Co.
Carlisle U. v Plymouth Arg.
Charlton Ath. v Bolton W.
Fulham v Blackburn R.
Luton T. v Blackpool
Nottingham F. v Bristol R.
Oldham Ath. v W.B.A.
Orient v Oxford U.
Southampton v Hull C.
Sunderland v Portsmouth
York C. v Chelsea

DIVISION THREE
Brighton & H.A. v Sheffield W.
Bury v Cardiff C.
Crystal Palace v Chesterfield
Grimsby T. v Gillingham
Halifax T. v Aldershot
Hereford U. v Rotherham U.
Mansfield T. v Colchester U.
Peterborough U. v Shrewsbury T.
Preston N.E. v Port Vale
Southend U. v Chester
Swindon T. v Walsall
Wrexham v Millwall

DIVISION FOUR
Barnsley v Southport
Bradford C. v Cambridge U.
Darlington v AFC Bournemouth
Doncaster R. v Tranmere R.
Hartlepool v Brentford
Huddersfield T. v Watford
Newport Co. v Workington
Reading v Crewe Alex.
Stockport Co. v Northampton T.
Swansea C. v Rochdale
Torquay U. v Lincoln C.